UNCREDIBLE THOUGHTS

(Essays, Spiels, and Poppycock)

by
John Marszalkowski

Copyright © 2019 by BARF-BAG PUBLISHING

All rights reserved. This book or any portion thereof may not be reproduced or used in any manner whatsoever without the express written permission of the publisher except for the use of brief quotations in a book review or scholarly journal.

First Printing: 2019

ISBN
Ebook   978-1-7320226-4-5
Paperback   978-1-7320226-5-2
Hardcover   978-1-7320226-6-9

BARF-BAG PUBLISHING
C/O ORPHONIC LLC
PO BOX 210454
MILWAUKEE WI 53221-8008
http://ThisIsAReal.Company

Ordering Information:
Special discounts are available on quantity purchases by corporations, associations, educators, and others. For details, contact the publisher at the above-listed address.

U.S. trade bookstores and wholesalers: Please contact Barf-Bag Publishing at the above-listed URL address.

UNCREDIBLE THOUGHTS
(Essays, Spiels, and Poppycock)

Author: John Marszalkowski

Foreword: Christy Hall Watson

Editor: Jessica Greenfield
Proofreader: Donna Marszalkowski
Beta-Readers: Oliver Nepper & Miranda Reads

Cover Photographer: Deni Storm Rodgers
Cover Designer: Jason Gierl
Book Designer: Mark Lalumondier
Chapter Photography: Jen Janviere
Illustrator: Em Seagle
Barf-Bag Logo: William Sutton

Dedication

This book is dedicated to the life of my brother, Brian Marshall.

I'll always remember how slighted he felt when he wasn't mentioned at all in my first book. I'm going to include a photo of him here, but don't worry, he's still alive.

Brian Marshall
Born 1968 - Still Alive 2019

Contents

Forward 1

Introduction................................ 5

Lucky For Us Ugly People,
Sex Doesn't Always Sell 11

My First Attempt at Fiction 19

Striving To Be Overweight................... 31

Esteem Will Rise 39

Math Class Could Have Been More Fun 45

Okay, Fine. Here's Another Attempt at Fiction. ... 51

I'm Just Here to Look at You................. 63

What Are You Selling? 69

Thou Shall Not Covet 77

Skunks 87

White History Month Shouldn't Exist......... 91

Your Unhappiness Is Stupid; Time For A Nap **97**

Assholes, And The Rest **99**

Do I Have A Mild Case Of Hoarding? **107**

Cassettes **111**

That One Time I Peed My Pants **117**

Tweets I've Tweeted on Twitter **119**

Everyone Is A Feminist Until Proven Jerks **127**

The Secret Message **133**

The Final Chapter **137**

Acknowledgments **147**

About The Author **149**

Foreword
by Christy Hall Watson

When I first met Johnny, way back in 2012, I didn't pay much attention to him. My mind simply logged him as looking like a professional who knew what he was doing. I wasn't being an asshole, at least not intentionally. It was my first time hosting The Moth's Milwaukee StorySlam, and I was so nervous I was trying not to vomit. Johnny was the videographer. I remember a brief introduction. I tend to get tunnel vision before a show, and I'm sure Johnny gave me direction or helpful advice but I have no idea what he said. He just knew what he was doing, which made me wonder if I knew what I was doing, so I'm sure I did whatever he may have told me to do.

It turns out Johnny is a pretty awesome guy. He is friendly, open, and kind. His wonderful first book, "Buy My Book, Not Because You Should, But Because I'd Like Some Money", had a release date and event scheduled for November 2018. Johnny remembered I was planning on writing a children's book, and in February of 2018, he told me he put my book on the launch bill, so I needed to get it done. It was the push I needed, a silent vote of confidence, and once again, inspired by his professionalism, a valid reason to complete my book. (The book "Martha Dreams of Dinosaurs" is available in both hardback and paperback on Amazon). He also included two other local writers in the event. It was a lot of fun, and quite successful. Had I set it up, I would have been a nervous wreck. Johnny isn't like that. He is easy going and really just trusts in the natural progress of things.

"Uncredible Thoughts" is a reflection of this trust. It reads like an adult Choose Your Own Adventure, which is how I believe Johnny lives his life. If he wants to start his own videography business, he does, and it is successful. If he wants to write and play music, he starts a band. If he wants to express himself through spoken word, he creates a fantastic podcast called "Who are We to Podcast". If he feels his creativity would be best expressed through the written word, he publishes books. He makes a decision and trusts in it. For all his self-depreciation, Johnny is quite the renaissance man and a pretty fantastic person. He embraces his ADHD and uses it not only to empathize with others but to create a book that works with it. Reading the book is like switching channels on the

Foreword by Christy Hall Watson

TV. Eventually, you will land on a chapter you are interested in. Not ready to read about the truth of advertising or samples of fictional work? Go right to the nature channel and read about skunks. There is a whole chapter on math that I skimmed because I went to art school and all the numbers made my head hurt.

This book reminds me of our chats in the green room. Occasionally before a show, Johnny would come into the green room, say hi to my husband and whoever else was in there, sit down and just start talking about a random topic. Sort of exploring out-loud thoughts that were in his head. I loved it. These brief explorations made my mind spark and got the energy flowing, which I believe made for a much better StorySlam. I'm still nervous before shows and the good vibes in the room that Johnny helped cultivate certainly helped me relax. Johnny spreads creativity and inspires people selflessly, whether in person, through his books or other ventures, and I'm not sure he even knows it.

Two days ago Johnny came backstage holding two extra-large pizzas. He had walked to a couple of places to get food for himself and our producer and decided to get food for everybody working the StorySlam that night. He refused to take money from myself and multiple other people. As we ate, we had another chat about random stuff, with each other and whoever wandered in and out of the green room. It was familiar, caring, comforting, informative, fun, and casual, just like it has been for the last 7 years. That's Johnny, and that's "Uncredible Thoughts".

Introduction

October 31st, 2018

Dear Diary,

Today I heard about something called NaNoWriMo. It's a novel-writing challenge where anyone can sign up to try and write a 50,000-word book in the month of November. I figure this is perfect since I don't have anything going on for most of November.

November 1st, 2018

Dear Diary,

I just wrote about 1700 words of fiction. It took all day and I didn't enjoy it at all. I don't think I can do this every day for 30 days. Or maybe I can, but I don't want to. I really don't want to.

November 2nd, 2018

Dear Diary,

Yeah, no. Fuck this. I prefer writing short rants. I hate dialog, character and story arcs, and plot in general. This is terrible. Today I tried writing a different story than the one I wrote yesterday. I tried going about it totally differently, but I still don't enjoy writing fiction. But I guess I'm glad I tried. I'm just going to do what I like doing, which is writing whatever weird thoughts I'm thinking in the same rant format I did for my last book.

Introduction

November 3rd, 2018

Dear Diary,

Holy shit, 1700 words a day is not easy, whether it's fiction or nonfiction. I don't think I can hold myself to this quota every single day. This isn't how my brain works. I'm going to take a day off to mentally rest.

November 15th, 2018

Dear Diary,

This was a terrible mistake.

Word count quotas are not how my brain excels. I get that this process might be important for a lot of writers that experience writers-block. I don't get writer's block. I believe that either you have something to write about, or you don't. If you don't have anything to say, don't say anything. Don't force yourself to write just so you can feel good about yourself. Write because something is in your head and it needs to come out. This is what I did with my first book, and I had absolutely no problem doing it.

I've decided to try and meet halfway. I'm giving myself a word-count goal of "whatever". I won't delete the fictional chapters, but I'm going to surround them with plenty of my normal ranty garbage.

December 1st, 2018

Dear Diary,

I failed the NaNoWriMo challenge and I do not care at all.

February 11th, 2019

Dear Diary,

It just occurred to me that the majority of this introduction has been a preface for my fiction chapters, and not really an introduction to the entire book.

All you really need to know about this book is that it was written by an ADHD mind that changes directions constantly and abruptly. Much like my first book, each chapter is independent and does not need to be read in order. If, while reading a different book, you've ever looked ahead and felt overwhelmed, then this book is for you. Each chapter is over before you know it. If you get bored with what you're reading, skip ahead to the next chapter; you're not missing anything.

Introduction

Like my first book, I might classify this book as humor, but don't look too hard for any jokes. The humor is simply where each individual might find it, and you might not find it anywhere. You will either laugh with me, at me, or not at all. I apologize that I feel the need to mask my genuine thoughts in a thin shroud of self-deprecation, but that's just how this book works.

February 19th, 2019

Dear Diary,

This is embarrassing to admit but I think I've been using the wrong book genre classifications for the last couple of years. When I started writing my first book, people would ask what kind of book it was. I would say something unofficial, like "a real shit-show." That's because terms like "memoir" or "autobiography" didn't seem to fit. What I always pictured for a memoir was a first-person true story with a beginning, middle, and end. Autobiographies were the same, but something that covered the highlights of an entire lifetime. My book would switch back and forth from true stories, opinions, rants, serious points, and subtle jokes. Memoirs and autobiographies just didn't seem like a perfect fit… but as far as I knew, there wasn't a better category to describe it.

While searching for popular books that resembled mine, I saw a term that I had only ever associated with homework: "Essays."

A quick internet search tells me this:

"Informal essays have no set structure and they are typically shorter than formal essays. Informal essays also use first and second person and often include thoughts and opinions. The subject matter of informal essays is brief and a subject does not explore the topic in depth." - *Some lady named Claire Bryant on Quora.com.*

Well, that sounds spot on.

Clearly, what I enjoy making are collections of informal essays. And so that is what this book is. Perhaps you knew all this already and it wasn't as mindblowing for you as it was for me. At least by sharing this realization I've helped tell you more about what to expect from this book. If you signed on with the expectation of an autobiography, memoir, or non-stop laughs, let me just recalibrate your expectations and say that this is instead a collection of essays, spiels, and poppycock.

Lucky For Us Ugly People, Sex Doesn't Always Sell

Being a Grimace-shaped man, I had always believed that the odds were stacked against me because I look like a dollop of sour cream. I believed I had a major obstacle to negotiate whenever convincing anyone of anything because the sight of me might make them feel like their genitals were about to cough out a cloud of sand. This obstacle included convincing people to listen to me, buy what I was selling, respect me, love me, and so on. I believed I was seeing constant proof in my life that "sex sells." I am finally starting to believe that my perspective was sometimes wrong, and sometimes only half right.

I worked a good number of years at a health club trying to convince people far healthier than myself that they needed to buy memberships and take nutritional supplements. I attributed my success to my excellent people skills but I felt that the more physically attractive salespeople had an advantage over me because of their looks. I mean, they did, but not for the reasons I thought they did. I thought people were buying from them because they were attracted to them, but sometimes it was that they wanted to BE them.

Let me set the scene: A husband and wife walk in and are interested in a tour of the gym. After the tour, they both sit down in the sales office with a hunky salesman. The husband notices his wife's speaking voice shift slightly in pitch, her posture adjust, her eyes locked, and suddenly he's convinced that she's daydreaming about doing body shots off of Hunky's six-pack. Is he filled with rage? No, he's too busy thinking about how much he needs a six-pack. He wants what Hunky has and the good news is Hunky is selling it.

This is what I call the "Rockstar Effect." When the audience at a rock concert is both men and women and the rockstar is a man, what happens is the women want to be WITH the rockstar and the men want to BE the rockstar. This is assuming everyone is a

Lucky For Us Ugly People, Sex Doesn't Always Sell

straight, cisgender horndog, and no one really cares about the music. Come to think of it, it's a terrible analogy. But you get the point. The point is that sex is selling only half the audience. Envy is selling the other half.

In my experience, my customers did not envy me or have any attraction to me, so all that was left was selling them on their own potential. I wasn't an example of the result, but if I could get their attention, I could talk them into picturing themselves as the result. No one hung on my every word because of how I looked, but sometimes my words were enough.

I never felt the "Rockstar Effect," even when I was in a rock band. Before, during, and after my days working at the gym, I was in a few bands. It was impossible to apply the "Rockstar Effect" analogy to an actual rock concert of mine because everyone at our shows were either members of the other bands, their girlfriends, or people who were more-or-less there just to be supportive. But there were other bands I knew that had large draws. And how did I account for the size of their crowd? Their attractive band members, obviously. It couldn't have possibly been their music. The "Rockstar Effect" could be applied to them for this reason.

Often in life, when I needed to compete for something like a client or a relationship, I would conclude that only sex sells and it determined the winners. Until now.

I've finally realized that sex only sells one thing: sex-related transactions. "Romance" (in its many forms), is really the only thing I can think of that sex sells. Here is how I reached that conclusion and what I call the "Worm on the Hook" method. I don't really call it that. It just felt weird to have a name for the first example and not have a name for the second. Since I'm being honest, I don't think I've ever said "The Rockstar Effect" or "Worm on the Hook Method" out loud even once before now. Anyway...

Nowadays we're being bombarded with advertising that is catered to our interests. The ads that pop up when we are scrolling through our favorite websites are carefully selected after studying our shopping habits and search engine history. Ads for things we are likely to buy are what we now see. Never before has advertising been this targeted. When many of us were kids, the television commercials only had one way to target audiences: The show you were watching. If you were watching after school cartoons, you were going to see a lot of toy ads. But that was about it. Pretty general. And so we could make assumptions about the ad's motivations. The girls in the bikinis for the beer

Lucky For Us Ugly People, Sex Doesn't Always Sell

ad that came on during the football game were trying to get the attention of red-blooded straight men. But did the girls in bikinis really sell the beer? Or did the close up of beer getting poured into the frosty mug sell the beer? Sex didn't sell, sex just got the attention. The beer sold the beer, I assume.

I saw sex selling in practice as a child watching TV, as a young adult selling gym memberships, and numerous times in between. I had pretty much accepted it as a fact of life, until recently.

Several months ago I started getting a lot of ads for yoga furniture in my Facebook feed. Yeah, yoga furniture. What the hell is that? I have no idea, besides the fact that the women in the ads are doing yoga while using these cushions. At least I assume it's yoga and not kama sutra positions. I would have no idea because I don't do yoga. I have no interest in buying anything yoga related. Yet, this company spends a lot of ad money on showing me their yoga pillows, or whatever they are. The reason for it is because I've clicked on their ads. Do you know why I clicked on them if I'm not interested in yoga furniture? It's because they were photos and videos of women doing yoga. Yeah, I clicked them. Many times. I'm not sorry. And no matter how much of an interaction I have with their marketing, I will never buy their products. Despite seeing their ads countless times, I can't even remember what their brand name is. Sex sold nothing. Sex cost them advertising money. The "Hey, look at this" part worked, but it sold nothing to me. The only thing I want to buy after seeing those ads is a copy of the kama sutra.

I can only speculate that half of the "Rockstar Effect" is happening and to the reversed genders. Perhaps the perfectly toned women in those ads represent WHO the customers want to be.

About a year or so ago I was in the market for a new mattress. I couldn't believe how many ads for different mattress companies bombarded my feed after just one web search. I bought one, and I continued to see the ads after. I remember thinking "What a waste… I get why I'm being targeted, but it's a shame the algorithms can't see that I bought one and am no longer in the market." No, I just kept seeing them. And I still see them. Know why? Because their ads ALWAYS feature videos of women with impossible legs in skimpy pajama shorts jumping onto mattresses in slow motion. Yeah, I click that shit every time. I can't help it. I took the bait, but what's the hook? If I hadn't just bought a new mattress, it might be hooking me on how interested I am in the product. But since I'm not interested in the product anymore, I'm just stealing the bait off the hook.

Lucky For Us Ugly People, Sex Doesn't Always Sell

In conclusion, sex only sells sex. It also gets A LOT of attention. Being an attractive person does not hurt your chances of getting people's attention. But you still need to do something with that attention. Otherwise, your audience is just stealing the bait off your line.

My First Attempt at Fiction

The following is a teaser to a fiction story I thought I might write. After writing a single chapter I decided that I hate writing fiction and I am not going to write the rest of the story.*

* However, if you like it and think it's deserving, feel free to finish writing it yourself.

Please send your constructive criticism to:

HATE MAIL, ℅ BARF-BAG PUBLISHING
PO BOX 210454, MILWAUKEE, WI 53221-8008

Okay, here goes nothing.

Rad Barlos

Rad had one of the most bewildering first names in his high school. Rad's name sounds pretty rad when interpreted to be a shortened version of radical. Unfortunately, it was short for Rhadamanthus, the longest name his parents must have been able to find in a list of Greek baby boy names. His friends left the "h" out when shortening it to Rad. However, never completely forgotten was his true full name, semiannually revisited with every new semester by new teachers reading off their attendance lists out loud.

"Rrrr... had-a-man-thus? Umm, Is there a Mr. Barlos here?"

"Here. Just Rad, please. Thank you."

A few giggles, but nothing too terrible. Was it because it was uncommon or because it sounded so long? It might have been 12 letters, but it was only 4 syllables. It's not like Olivia Blom had the same problem. No one called her Liv, always the full O-liv-i-a. Her name had a phenetic grace about it. He thought it felt pleasing to just say her name. His name was just weird.

My First Attempt at Fiction

Rad wasn't popular, but he was often mistaken for being so. Everyone had heard his name at some point, and it stuck. If someone asked, "Do you know Rad?" the answer was almost always "Oh, yeah, sure!" When in fact, very few people knew him well. He experienced a lonely variation of high school celebrity status, which was that everyone seemed to know who he was, but almost everyone didn't care.

Rad had a couple of good friends that knew him well. He was close to his family. He wanted to be liked as much as anyone, but it's not like he had any ambitions of being voted class president. He was mostly content. Mostly, because like many teenage boys, Rad definitely wanted to be well known by at least one person: Olivia Blom. It seemed no amount of social networking, messaging, or even talking directly to her could get him to register on her charming radar. After trying for the entire school year, his only conclusion was that she simply didn't care about the things he said. As a result, he tried extremely hard to sound more interesting than he thought he was.

"Did you ever notice that young kids have this undying love for building forts?" Rad said, standing in the lunch line directly behind Olivia.

UNCREDIBLE THOUGHTS

"What?" She said, startled. She wasn't even facing him.

"I distinctly remember my love for draping blankets over stacked couch cushions as an attempt to make a tent when I was a small child." he continued, to the back of her head before she turned to face him.

"Yeah, all kids do that." she replied, looking at him for a moment before looking away just enough to break eye-contact.

Rad looked off into the distance, recalling a memory. "The greatest gift I ever received as a kid was when my parents bought a new refrigerator, and I got the giant box it came in. It was the best fort. Room to play with all my action figures and tall enough to sit up straight. I even fit a small TV inside."

"That sounds normal for a little kid." Olivia said. She glanced up to the front of the line, half-turned away. They took half-steps forward as the line dragged along.

Suddenly snapping back to reality from his refrigerator box memories, he said "Yeah, that's what I'm saying. All kids do that. And a good chunk of them still have a desire to have a treehouse or something when they get a little older."

My First Attempt at Fiction

She nodded. "Everyone wants a place to call their own, I guess." She reached forward to grab a lunch-tray, but Rad had reached past her and handed one to her.

Once again talking to the back of her head, "Yeah but most kids have bedrooms. That never seems to be good enough. There is always a desire to build a new space someplace. Maybe we are like beavers and we have an instinctive urge to build dams."

She turned to face the lunch lady, glanced to see he was staring directly at her, and said, "I guess that makes sense."

"But then why is it that this natural urge, that almost all children seem to have, translates into so few careers of people constructing homes and stuff? There are a lot of architects and construction workers, but it's gotta be such a tiny percentage of all the jobs out there."

Olivia squinted for a moment and said, "That's because people decide there are other careers that they want to pursue. They have other passions in life."

Rad, not observing her reaction, continued. "Yeah, but, like, birds don't get to decide that they like catching worms more than building a nest. They have to do both."

"Human societies have economies." Olivia said, looking off into the distance. Rad was too focused on the closing remarks he was about to say, to notice that Olivia's words trailed off and she was no longer paying any attention to him.

"Yeah, but I'm just surprised that most people with a natural instinct to build dwellings would push that aside to instead do something else. Do our natural instincts fade over time in a society that negates our need to utilize them, or do we convince ourselves that an industry like advertising is natural?"

Rad waited in silence. Would she finally find something he said interesting?

She looked at him for a moment. The look on her face reflected the fact that she hadn't heard anything he just said and she responded with an extremely neutral statement: "You're weird." She flashed a small smile at him, paid for her lunch, and walked away.

The smile was confusing because while it seemed like she had no interest in him or his thoughts, she didn't completely ignore him. Was the smile just her being polite?

Rad was convinced that pretty much every thought in his head and every word that he spoke must either be meaningless, or he must sound like an idiot. It seemed the only person that cared about what he was saying was Lucas. As Rad sat down at the lunch table with Lucas and his other friends, he was warmly greeted with wide-eyed smiles and salutations.

"Hey, Rad! How's it going?" asked Lucas, who stopped eating and almost stood up at the arrival of his friend.

Rad sat down. "Hey, guys. What's up?"

"I saw you talking to Olivia in the lunch line." Lucas said with a tone of voice that was halfway between teasing and honest curiosity.

"Barely." Rad laughed.

"Yeah, it didn't look like it was going well."

Rad got defensive. "What do you mean?"

His friends looked around at each other for some kind of confirmation from each other that they weren't the only ones that noticed. "Did she even look at you? It looked like you were talking to yourself."

"Yeah, she looked at me. You don't know what you're talking about." Rad laughed uncomfortably. "Actually, she even smiled at me. But you're right, she didn't seem to care much for--"

UNCREDIBLE THOUGHTS

Lucas, eager to rejoice in any efforts Rad made, interrupted "Hey, she probably just forgot to take her pills today. A smile is a good start, right?"

Rad wasn't sure what he meant by that, but Lucas was right: A smile *was* a good start.

They started to eat. Between bites, Rad made small talk. "Are you guys all going to be at practice tonight?"

Rad's school, Eastwater High, had the world's worst track & field team. They had no trophies in the school lobby's case. No plaques. No recognition whatsoever. The school seemed to be so ashamed of the track & field team's performance, that most of the students didn't even know Eastwater *had* a track & field team. It didn't help that on more than one occasion the team photo was "mistakenly" left out of the yearbook. It was within this abomination of a sports team that Rad Barlos was a god among young men. A consistent winner of sprints, long jumps, and pole vaults, Rad had a nice collection of medals. But much like the relay races that he participated in, it seemed almost impossible to compensate enough to make up for his teammates. In Eastwater High's case, the weakest link was everyone on the team that wasn't Rad. One of the worst athletes in Eastwater history was Rad's best friend, Lucas. Lucas was a portly young man, despite his constant activity. Lucas looked up to Rad, and Rad... well, Rad respected Lucas and enjoyed his company. Despite Rad's undeniable success in track, his accomplishments went fairly unknown amongst his classmates.

Reminded by Rad's question, Lucas' eyes lit up. "Oh, man. I forgot to tell you about this morning! It was the worst!"

"What happened?"

"My mom made this awesome breakfast because my brother is in town visiting."

"That sounds terrible." Rad said sarcastically.

"No, the breakfast was great! Pancakes, eggs, sausage, bacon, toast, cereal, French toast, orange juice... It was a real buffet!"

"What did you have?"

"All of it."

"What?"

"Yeah, dude, a little bit of everything."

"How did you get to school?"

"The same way I always do. I ran."

UNCREDIBLE THOUGHTS

"You ran? Like, a slow jog?"

"Naw, man, I spent a lot of extra time eating breakfast, so I had to make up that time running."

"Oh no..."

"Yeah man, that was the worst part."

"Running as fast as you could with a full stomach? I bet."

"Naw, dude. I got to class and got in the door with, like, a second to spare, and immediately barfed that glorious breakfast into the garbage can at the front of the room with everyone watching."

"Oh man, that had to be embarrassing!"

"The worst part was afterward, sitting at my desk, knowing that I almost had it all. Just thinking about it over and over. The perfect breakfast, at the bottom of that garbage bag, being hauled away by the janitor. I was left with nothing. I tried to have it all, and instead, I was hungry by the end of the first period. It just goes to show you."

"What? It goes to show you what?"

"I don't know. I was hoping someone else could decipher a moral from that story." Lucas said as he shoveled his lunch into his mouth.

They all laughed until eventually, Rad said, "It sounds like we need to feed you before the next track meet if you're making record time running with a full stomach."

They all chuckled as Lucas slapped his hand down on Rad's shoulder. "Maybe you're right, brother."

They felt a legitimate brotherhood between them that just didn't make any sense to Rad. They all cared about each other, talked about anything and everything, and they were always glad to see one another. Rad appreciated his friends but what he didn't understand was why they appreciated him. They clearly didn't know what Oliva Blom knew, which was that there was nothing worth knowing about Rad Barlos, besides his name.

Striving To Be Overweight

I was asked to write about this subject by my friend, Erica. It almost hurts to write it, because I had dreams of the subject being its own separate book. That could still happen, I guess. In that case, consider this a sample.

Here goes nothing.

A weight loss journey is not a single race; it's a series of races. Each race has its own finish line. You deserve to acknowledge that you've completed a goal; not just passing a milestone on your way to somewhere else. The truth is there is no finish line if health is a single journey. The finish moves forward as you go, and you will never finish trying to be finished. This is no way to get motivated about going in the right direction. It's just too overwhelming to try and accomplish a task so large that it can never be completed. Especially for someone with ADHD, like myself.

I won't speak for what works for other people, but I've had the most luck breaking sizable tasks into a bunch of smaller tasks.

By the way, please forgive my "race" analogy. I'm not suggesting you need to run races. I like the "finish line" analogy and they kind of go hand-in-hand. I'm not trying to imply that any of these "races" require speed or competition with others. Just trying to emphasize the importance of it having a clear ending.

I wanted to write a book to emphasize the significance of how extraordinarily amazing it is for someone to start a race as an "obese" person and cross the finish line as "overweight." If you're not familiar with Body Mass Index (BMI), it has the following categories:

- Underweight : < 18.5
- Normal : 18.5-24.9
- Overweight : 25-29.9
- Obese, class 1 : 30-34.9

- Obese, class 2 : 35-39.9
- Obese, class 3 : 40+

Obese, class 3 is also refered to as "Morbidly Obese."

You can figure out what number you are by multiplying your weight in pounds by 703 and then dividing that amount by your height in inches squared.

Example: A "normal" 6-foot person weighing 160-pounds has a BMI of 21.7
$(160 \times 703)/(72^2)=21.7$

Notice that there isn't a category called "healthy." You either weigh **way** too much, too much, too little, or you're in the goldilocks zone of just "normal."

BMI has received a lot of criticism from pretty much ...everyone, because it's ...terrible. I've interviewed a couple MD's and several other health professionals and here is a summary of their opinions: BMI is an okay way to track an entire population's weight, or risks based on averages, but it's not a good way to track an individual's health. When you want to figure out which US state is the fattest, for example, you don't measure everyone's individual body fat percentages. You use BMI. BMI doesn't take into account each individual's body type, body fat, gender, age, or almost any of the things that dramatically affect your weight. It's a lazy way to look at a group of three-million people and determine that Mississippi takes first place for plumpness. It's also a lazy way for your life insurance company to guess how likely it is that you'll die early (so they can charge you more). It's how doctors place their bets on how likely it is people will get cancer or have heart disease. All averages without looking at individuals. What I'm saying is that we use BMI to measure individuals anyway, even though the results have very little to do with an individual's health. I'll try to cut to the chase. This is just a sample, after all.

Finish lines have to mean something beyond a unit of measurement: To you, to those holding you accountable, and to society in general. I believe they have to invoke a "completed" feeling, not a "you're not there yet" feeling. That's how you appreciate the value of them. If you are morbidly obese, your health is (most likely) poor. You are (on average) more likely to suffer from a variety of diseases. It is (probably) in your best interest to not be morbidly obese. However, for many who are, it is an overwhelming task to attempt when the finish line is "normal." It's enough to give up before you even start.

I'm not the first person to suggest that starting is better than doing nothing. I'm not the first person to write about how a single pound lost is the first of many to follow, and so on. I'm not the first to write about anything health related, I'm sure. But I think there needs to be a movement that celebrates many finish lines and separates them from milestones. Just semantics, really. A milestone tells you how far you've come, but you're not there yet. A finish line says "You did it! Congratulations! If you want to, there are more races out there… but today, you have completed something."

What is that "something" that you completed? It's different for everyone, but for me it has to mean something beyond a unit of measurement. For me, specifically, that meaningful moment is crossing over from being "obese" to "overweight." Simply, not being obese anymore. That means something. Yes, it's still a measurement. However, it's a measurement that holds purpose in this world. Your doctor tells you that your risk of x has decreased by y%. Your insurance gets cheaper. From a health perspective, you are in a different category now. How is that not a major accomplishment? How is that not worthy of a celebration? For those that do it, it might be the single most important thing they've done for themselves in their entire lives. And yet, it will be treated as the following by many people: "Good job, you're part way there." How heartbreaking is that? They just completed a very difficult challenge, and society tells them they aren't done yet.

Maybe it's a psychological problem and not a numbers problem. The difference between obese and overweight is one-tenth of a pound. For me (5'8"), it's dropping from 197-pounds down to 196.9 to cross the finish line. Is a 197-pound person any more unhealthy than the same person at 196.9? I would say not. But this difference still MEANS something. Even if it's on the loathed BMI chart.

The book I almost wrote would have been titled "Striving To Be Overweight (A Weightloss Story)" because it wouldn't be about trying to be "normal." Long before reaching "normal" a major victory has to take place, and that's reaching "overweight." And it's no simple feat. It could be one of the hardest things a person does in their life. And something that significant just can't be shrugged off as a milestone... As a "you're almost there." No! Fuck that! You did it! You did what others might call impossible. You did what you might have thought was impossible. That is not a milestone. That is the fucking finish line to a very tough race, and you completed it. The next race is out there, if you want it. But not today. Today you are a winner of a race that is over.

And to go from morbidly obese to only overweight is a journey that contains a few finish lines along the way. Finish lines, not milestones. The same way getting

Striving To Be Overweight

down to overweight is a victory that takes place long before ever reaching normal, going from class 3 to class 2, or class 2 to class 1, is a major accomplishment that must happen FIRST. For someone my height, class 2 to class 1 means losing 33-pounds. That's a lot of pounds. Shouldn't that be a finish line? You've finished the class 2 obesity race, you've crossed the finish line, and whenever you feel like it (if you even feel like it) the class 1 obesity race is out there.

It's inspiring to me to imagine that finish line. Like I said before, I almost made it once. I was 274 pounds and with a variety of exercises and militant diet, I lost 69 pounds in one year.* I was so close. Only 8.1 pounds more, and I could have had the confidence to write that damn book. Instead, I celebrated a milestone of 205, took a break, and ...well, that's a different story for another book.

*In case you're wondering, I did the "Couch to 5K" program to train for my first 5K run. The entire process was terrible, save one thing: great friends. I couldn't have done it without Ingrid, Erica, and Steve (we named our running group P.A.T.H. which stood for Pathetic Attempts Toward Health). I also was attending Brazilian Jiu Jitsu a couple times a week and trying to get ready for a tournament. The 205 milestone was actually the weight division I wanted to compete in. To be fully transparent, I was probably naturally 215 with a 10-pound water-cut. On top of the exercise, I tried a lot of different diets over that time, and I was pretty strict about whatever I was doing 90% of the time.

Esteem Will Rise

No, I didn't think of that. It's a lyric from a great song with almost the same title (Steam Will Rise) by the band Silverchair.

I just wanted to type for a minute about self-esteem. Yes, I've done this in the past, but I have a feeling I'll be revisiting the subject for the rest of my life.

Back in high school, and for a short amount of time after, I loved seeing photos of myself. In the early years of high school, no one had digital cameras yet. Photography students would be seen shooting with manual film cameras, but I often had a cheap camera with me. Loaded in that junk camera was a roll of Fuji 100 speed 35mm film. It would take about 12 pictures before it was done. Then I'd take those photos to Walgreens, where I'd have to wait an entire day or two to see if any of them looked satisfactory at all. It seemed like 1-hour photo delivery got popular while I was in high school and by my senior year, my buddy Kenneth had a digital camera (he was most likely the only one who did). We didn't have the instant gratification that the selfie generation has, and you couldn't take unlimited shots, so if a photo was developed that had your face in it, and you liked that photo, that was truly something special.

I know of one photo I took in a mirror; a selfie, years before anything would ever be called that. I liked it, I guess. I liked pretty much any photo of me, though. I liked to make goofy faces as well as normal ones. I liked having my photo taken with my friends. It was very rare that I'd see a photo of myself that I didn't want anyone to see. It was either a great photo, or it was amusing because it wasn't a great photo. Nothing ever seemed to be unflattering... even if it was, that wasn't how I saw the photos. And when it was time to pick them up from the developer at Walgreens, I was always excited to see myself.

What happened to that narcissism? Where did that self-love go? Yeah, I got fat, but so what? Why are

Esteem Will Rise

the fat photos not funny, the way unflattering skinny photos used to be? Why is it that I can't stand the sight of myself anymore? I can still listen to my music. I suppose the music is from years ago. I like hearing myself talk on my podcast episodes. I enjoy reading my own writings. There are clearly parts of myself that I like. I often say that "I hate myself" but that's not true. I obviously like some things about myself. But why do I hate my obesity so much? I'm not asking, "how do I solve the problem of my obesity?" But why does my obesity bring so much self-hatred?

I've never been very muscular. There were times when I was leaner than others. But I never had "I'm proud of my muscles" muscles. However, I have never looked at a photo of myself when I was skinnier and been ashamed at the lack of biceps or traps. The old photos didn't show anything I was proud of. I just didn't hate the sight of myself.

It seems to me that obesity isn't the problem. It's not the root of the problem, anyway. To quote Eugene Lee Yang, "If you have a problem with how you look, that's a way deeper issue than just changing your outsides."

Self esteem was so easy to find back when I was younger. These days, it's a bit harder. I have to go looking for it, and it's not where I left it.

UNCREDIBLE THOUGHTS

Today I was reflecting on my history of over-listening to my own songs. It is normal to get sick of your own music from countless rehearsals, endless recording takes, and never-ending mixing listens. A good chunk of those are scanning for mistakes or errors, so that they can be fixed before the public hears them. Whether you're editing your writings or judging your nearly completed painting, whatever you're making needs to be reviewed thoroughly. We do this to make sure the finished version is as perfected as possible, within the parameters of our expectations.

What are our expectations of what is good enough? When it came to writing songs, I knew that I would be judged when they were heard. I wasn't the best singer or the strongest guitarist, so I might have had slightly low standards for what passed as "good enough." But what did pass was a polished version of something that started off much more scuffed. In the end, I was proud of it. And because of that, I listened to it a lot. Not just the required over-listening, but even more over-listening. I would get burned out listening to it, but I never stopped. My wife (Desiree) played bass on all those recordings, and she was absolutely sick of them in no time. She originally liked all the songs, but I think she'd be happy never hearing any of them ever again. I'm different.

Esteem Will Rise

When a song I've written randomly pops up in the shuffle of our music library, I don't turn it off unless Dez is in the room. I listen to it again. I pretend I'm someone else listening to it, and then I judge myself. Not in a negative way, necessarily. I'm not thinking "Oh man, you suck." I'm usually thinking something like "I was a better guitarist back then" or "I probably can't hit that note anymore." To the contrary, I suppose I judge my past positively, as long as in doing so it shits on me currently.

Similarly, I went through almost the same process writing my first book. I'd write a paragraph, stop, reread, make changes. I'd finish a chapter, I'd reread, I'd make changes. I'd finish the second chapter, I'd reread both chapters, and make changes to both. I did (what I think is) a normal amount of self-critiquing, and rereading. But even after that, after the whole book was written and edited and proofread, I reread it again. Not as a chore or to try and spot mistakes (I *was* trying to spot mistakes), but mainly because I enjoyed reading what I wrote. How vain is that? I set out to make a book that an idiot like myself might enjoy, and I did enjoy it. I still do. Yeah, I'm sick of reading it, but if I start reading part of it now, I'll keep going. I love my own writing. And I know it's not great. I know that people can judge it and judge me, but it fits into those parameters of what I expect it to be, and I think, relative to those expectations, it's perfect.

UNCREDIBLE THOUGHTS

I think the problem with how I see myself when I look in the mirror is that my body and my health do not fit into the parameters of what I expect it to be. Right now, relative to what my expectations are, I'm so far from perfect that I hate myself. Should I move the bar of expectations? Should I challenge myself to try and reach it? Maybe I can start by meeting it halfway.

Math Class Could Have Been More Fun

It is my firm belief that if Math had been taught to me as word problems in high school, the way math equations were often done in elementary school, then I might have actually enjoyed the puzzle that is algebra. Instead, algebra in my late twentieth century high school and early twenty-first century college was the memorization of procedures with cold boring numbers that didn't represent anything. Solving a number equation was a chore. Solving a word problem was a puzzle. Puzzles are games. Chores are work. You get the idea.

I wouldn't learn for another 10 years that I might actually enjoy solving the riddles in algebra, but I've yet to find a format that meets my expectations. Consequently, I have started making my own equations, in hopes that if you like them, and know where I can find more, you can reach out to me and point me in the right direction.

The Venue

You live in a city that doesn't have a non-profit all-age music venue. You decide to create it. The problem is getting the perfect ratio of expense to income.

Some expenses include:

- $1.25 per square foot for rent and utilities per month
- $4000 per month for staff, insurance, and other things.

Market research tells you that you can plan for having many events per month. However, Saturdays are likely to have the highest attendance. This means that you should plan to cover all your expenses with at least 4 popular events per month. $10 seems to be the highest ticket price that's realistic for the types of bands that are willing to work for a percentage of ticket sales without a guaranteed rate; that amount being 50% of admission collected.

The fire-code says that you must have 7-square-feet of space for each person in attendance to sit or stand. There is a lot of space in the room where people can't stand, such as the stage, storage area, and bathrooms. The stage and storage will be 200-square-feet. The bathrooms end up being 50-square-feet for every 15-people.

The landlord owns a very large warehouse and is offering to build out a space for your venue. You get to choose how many square feet you need. Use the above info to choose a size that will be just big enough to hold enough people to cover the costs with 4 shows a month. Build it oversized and your risk and costs will be too high. Build it too small and it won't hold enough paying customers to cover costs.

(For the record, this is a fun math problem; Not an exact science of non-profit venue management and finance.)

Your Answer: _____

The Price Tag

An online retailer really wants to have nice and neat prices on their products. They want to include the cost of shipping, sales tax, and the transaction fee in the price. For invoicing purposes, the retailer needs to come up with a price first, before added taxes and fees.

- Shipping is a flat amount of $4.70
- The sales tax is 5.6% of the entire transaction.
- The transaction fee is $0.30 + 2.9% of the entire transaction.
- To be clear: the transaction fee applies to the item, *the tax*, and shipping ...AND the tax applies to the item, *the transaction fee*, and shipping.

If the retailer wants the final price of an item to be exactly $100 for the client, then how much does that item need to be priced at BEFORE shipping, sales tax, and the fee is added?

What formula can the retailer use to figure out the prices of other amounts?

Your Answer: _____

In Conclusion

Sorry, there is no answer key. These are puzzles and you're welcome to try and figure them out. In case I wasn't clear before, I really have NO IDEA how to do math. I failed math class. I don't even know if these word problems ARE algebra! I'm just saying that a lot of people learn differently, and stuff like this would have gotten me more interested in the subject.

Okay, Fine. Here's Another Attempt at Fiction.

I really hated writing that first fiction chapter, "Rad Barlos." I asked myself why, and I think it might have been because I was trying to write some Young Adult story about high schoolers. Why did I choose that? I don't know, it's a formula that works for other people. Not so much for me, though.

That's why I'm going to try something different for this next story. Just like the other fiction chapter, if you like this, feel free to just take it and finish it yourself. I enjoyed dreaming up this character and this scenario, but I don't have a larger story to tell you.

The Owner

It has been an amazing past few years, Peter thought. He had come into money. Not just money, but an obscene amount of wealth. His evil uncle's company was the world's largest manufacturer of weapons for war, so after he died and Peter inherited everything, he dissolved the company for one enormous cashiers check. After months of reflection, he decided what to do with it and himself. He started the world's largest manufacturer of clothespins, and he named it "Global Clamp Solutions, Inc." He hired a lawyer, and proceeded to buy out every company that manufactured little wooden clothespins. And just like that, Peter was the owner of the largest corporate conglomerate of clothespin manufacturers in the world.

"Why clothespins?" everyone would ask. His answer was always the same, "It's my passion." How could a man have a passion for a wooden clamp that secured wet laundry to a clothesline and kept potato chip bags shut? Everyone assumed it was a passion for manufacturing, a need to make something tangible, or simply a desire to manage people. No, it was none of those things. It was a passion for absolutely nothing, which manifested itself in an international clothespin conglomerate.

Okay, Fine. Here's Another Attempt at Fiction.

Peter arrived at the downtown corporate headquarters. He took a limo to work every day, because why not? The doorman greeted him by name, but the elevator operator nodded while trying to not look Peter directly in the eye. Peter was unsure if the elevator operator was shy, didn't like Peter, or if not talking to him was some form of respect. This was all new to Peter, so he just went with the flow. The problem was that the building was old, so it was a very long, quiet trip up to the 89th floor.

Peter stepped out of the elevator, walked through the glass doors and was immediately greeted by three employees. The office receptionist simply said "Good morning, Mr. Williams." His personal secretary said "Mr. Williams, I rescheduled your morning meetings, but Ms. Miller won't be able to attend the rescheduled appointment." To which a half-listening Peter replied "Hmm? Cool. Err, I mean, that's fine." Peter was still getting used to seeing this "thing" he had built. The sight of it always stole most of his attention when he walked in. The third person to greet him was an intern who simply took his coat. Peter had no idea what his name was. Peter often tried to start a conversation, but the intern was quick to get out of the way.

The office had an established flow that Peter was trying to fit himself into. The former businesses that Peter had bought and combined were respectively well-oiled machines, and Peter brought no new innovations to how they operated. He was just their uniter.

Peter shut the door to his corner office after he was inside. He closed the blinds to the window facing the bullpen and walked across the room slowly. He dragged his fingers across the smooth leather sofa. Of all the things he had obtained over the last few years, this leather sofa was one of the things that he appreciated the most. Mainly because it was a piece of leather furniture his cat, Mr. Pickles, couldn't destroy. If someone saw Peter's home and then his office, they would never guess they belonged to the same person. That sofa was Peter's new professional image, while the torn and stained couch at home was who he really was.

Peter walked between the chairs facing the front of his large mahogany desk. He slowed his pace even more to enjoy the journey to the other side. His chair was leather, like his prized sofa, only he had broken this chair in over the last several months. It had character now, and it was the most comfortable desk chair Peter had ever sat in. On most days he would sit in it all day long, and never feel uncomfortable. As perfect as his broken-in chair was, Peter still enjoyed looking across the room at his beloved virgin-skinned sofa. No one ever sat on it, mostly because it was rare that anyone

Okay, Fine. Here's Another Attempt at Fiction.

went in his office that didn't remain standing and leave shortly after entering.

The walls showcased a few expensive pieces of art that he was told were valuable. Next to them, in an expensive frame, hung Peter's high school diploma. Peter got the idea from the other executives who had displayed their business degrees in their offices.

Peter almost sat down, before he realized he didn't have a coffee yet. He knew he could just ask an intern to get one for him, but he enjoyed walking to the breakroom so he could interact with his staff.

While walking through the various departments, he stopped to wave through the window into the office of his director of management, Camilla Miller. He didn't stop to chat because he didn't like to distract her. She always seemed so busy. Camilla had a lot of responsibility, but Peter wasn't entirely sure what she was doing that made her so busy. She was basically the boss of all the different factory directors. The factory directors were the bosses of the factory's operation managers. The operation managers were the bosses of the shift managers, and the shift managers managed their teams of employees. The way Peter saw it, problems should be solved by managers long before they reached Camilla. However, Camilla was very involved. Peter could see why his recruitment team picked her. Besides, Peter really didn't know much about how management worked.

He liked to stop by the marketing department to catch up with them, though. They would talk about last night's football game, or what new show they should binge-watch. He knew they weren't busy, because what do those people actually do, really? Especially marketing for clothespins. Peter couldn't remember the last time he saw an ad for clothespins before he took over. Whatever it is they had on their plate for the day, they had time to take a break and talk to him.

Peter walked into the break room and stared blankly at the espresso machine. He had no idea how to use it. Usually what would happen was other people would be in there using it, he would get in line, and someone would make his latte for him. He never actually realized this, because he would be distracted by his conversations with everyone. However, today no one was in the break room. He had no idea how the machine worked, so he quickly left.

He walked back into his office and opened the blinds so he could see out onto the entire floor of desks and people. He thought about how such a small task felt like such a big change. Closed blinds turned his office into a private, but lonely, cell. Open blinds washed away the loneliness instantly. Peter left the door open

Okay, Fine. Here's Another Attempt at Fiction.

just to let the sound of people and movement flood his space. He never felt lonely here, surrounded by so many people. They were all independent and didn't seem to need his leadership. Yet, they always stopped what they were doing to listen to his advice and ideas. The dynamic was perfect for Peter.

He walked over to his diploma and stared at the calligraphy of his name while he reached into the mini-refrigerator in front of him to grab a soda. This corner of his office was originally supposed to be a classy dry bar, but it quickly grew. Apparently not everyone was a whiskey drinker, so he had to expand his selection of liquor. He was able to figure out what everyone liked by his frequent visits out to the floor. Peter understood the need for variety, as even he didn't like whiskey. He just had it because that's what he thought he was supposed to have. What he really liked were sweet brandy old fashioneds. That's why he got the mini-fridge; so he could keep cold soda and cherries on hand. However, since Peter didn't like drinking cocktails alone, he just kept drinking all his soda.

He sat in his impossibly comfortable chair, turned on his computer, and loaded his email. He had a pretty full inbox, but very few emails that he wasn't simply cc'd on. He glanced through them all. They were mostly directors messaging each other, and keeping him in the loop of their conversation. Peter liked to sometimes reply-all to them with a relevantly clever meme, but as far as the conversations went, he didn't have much to add. He had a great team, and they seemed to have everything under control. Having nothing urgent to deal with in his email, he switched windows and spent the next few hours perusing social media sites.

Realizing his lemon lime soda was caffeine free, and without his usual latte, Peter decided to stretch his legs and get a coffee from the cafe downstairs in the building lobby. Peter took a sharp right out his door and stopped at his secretary's desk.

"Hey Denise. I'm going to get a coffee from downstairs. Do you want anything?"

"No, thank you, Mr. Williams. Don't forget, you have that rescheduled meeting with the directors right after lunch today."

"What is the meeting about?"

"It's the monthly factory productivity evaluations."

"Meh, they don't really need me for that, do they? Who they really need is Camilla. Did you say she wasn't available?"

Okay, Fine. Here's Another Attempt at Fiction.

"That's correct. Ms. Miller will be flying to the Houston factory this afternoon."

"Oh, that's a shame. See if they can reschedule it again before she leaves. I'll just sit this one out."

"Where will you be, so I can update your schedule?"

"Well, I'm going to start with getting that coffee, and see where it goes from there."

Peter walked toward the elevator. As he opened the glass door to exit the offices, a woman walked in. She asked "Hi, is this the Global Clamp Solutions' corporate headquarters?"

"Yes, ma'am. What can I help you with?"

"I have an interview at eleven-thirty. I'm meeting with Mr. O'Donnell--"

The office receptionist quickly interjected "Hello Ms. Jones. Please feel free to have a seat and Mr. O'Donnell will be with you shortly."

"Oh, nonsense." said Peter. "I'll introduce you to Jim. He's right over here." He led her over to James O'Donnell's desk in the Human Resources office.

"Hey Jim, your eleven thirty is here. This is... Ms. Jones, I didn't catch your first name." Peter said.

"Ms. Jones is fine."

"Oh! Okay, fair enough." Peter laughed nervously.

"Thank you very much, Mr. Williams. Ms. Jones, please allow me to introduce you to the owner of Global Clamp Solutions, Mr. Peter Williams. Mr. Williams, this is--"

"My name is Mary! I'm so sorry, Mr. Williams! I--"

"Oh, no, it's all good! I'm sorry... I'm still getting used to all this last name stuff. No worries." Peter interrupted.

Mr. O'Donnell interjected, "I'm sure you're very busy Mr. Williams. Thank you for bringing Ms. Jones over."

"Yes, and I'm sorry again--" Ms. Jones tried to apologize, but Peter again interrupted,

"Call me Peter. Mr. Williams is my dog's name."

Ms. Jones smiled. "Your dog has the same last name as you?"

"No... I don't know why I said that. I don't have a dog. I have a cat. His name is Mr. Pickles." Peter said.

Okay, Fine. Here's Another Attempt at Fiction.

"Well, Peter, it sounds like you're comfortable calling pets, both real and imaginary, by their last names. But you can call me Mary."

"No, no, you're right. I gotta get the hang of this professional stuff. It's Ms. Jones. You're right. Okay, I'll get out of your hair. Good luck with the interview."

"Thank you." Mary said.

Mr. O'Donnell added "Yes, thank you, Mr. Williams."

"Jimmy, make sure you hire her, okay?"

Mr. O'Donnell let out a sigh he failed to conceal and said, "I'm sure the interview will go well, sir."

Peter walked out to the elevators again. The doors opened, and the elevator operator nodded and looked straight forward.

"Lobby please." Peter said. He was about to stand quietly for the journey downstairs but decided to mix things up today. "What's your name?"

"Sir?"

"Your name. My name is Peter. Or Mr. Williams. Or Peter Williams. Or Shit-head. Whatever feels right."

"Yes, Mr. Williams."

Peter spent the rest of the ride in silence. He thought he may never get used to the formalities and class etiquette. Did he really want all of this? Of course he did, or at least parts of it, anyway. He has a gorgeous leather sofa in a place his cat will never destroy it. A place where he can go every day and talk to people. Not friends, necessarily, but people that talked to him at least. A place with delicious coffee, a mini bar, and a really comfortable chair where he could sit on the internet all day and look busy doing whatever he felt like. And now, Ms. Mary Jones, who might be another reason to look forward to coming in to work. Clothespins? Not a passion. Hard work? Not interested. Being in the office, and without anyone there able to tell him he couldn't be, was his only desire.

I'm Just Here to Look at You.

There is an interesting phenomenon that I've noticed happening with myself that has only existed in the second half of my life. This phenomenon is my desire to look at pictures of people that I don't really know on the internet. Nothing indecent and not complete strangers, but rather just normal looking photos of everyday life from people in social circles I share. People I've met somewhere between twice and never. Am I "friends" with these people on social media? Yes. But if they asked me why, the answer I'd be too embarrassed to give is "I'm just here to look at you."

UNCREDIBLE THOUGHTS

I'm not totally sure how normal this is. It's a digital equivalent to people-watching, I suppose. People have always watched each other in passing. Totally normal; so long as you don't look like you're staring. You're totally staring, but you can't look like you are. That would be rude. But stare at someone and don't get caught? Not rude.

Nevertheless, I've realized that there are people I follow on social media that might not necessarily add value to my life in any way I'd like to admit. They are people that I met or intended to meet through some form of relevant interaction that warranted staying connected, but in time just became a connection that I look at. I could list names, but that might get awkward real fast. I'll list some example scenarios, though.

For about five years of my life, my photography & video business was my number one priority. Part of the job involved networking, as a lot of business was referrals and word of mouth. The more vendors I could meet, the better. What started out as strictly business strategy ended up morphing into something else: real friendships. Today I'm not nearly as involved in the wedding industry as I was seven years ago, but I'm still good friends with several people that I met in that context. When I say good friends, I mean real friends. People I get a beer with and hangout with outside of the context of work. People who visited

I'm Just Here to Look at You.

Desiree and me at the hospital when Charlotte was born. You know, real friends. The friendship may have a work-foundation, but it's still a real friendship. I obviously want to stay connected with those people. But I'm also connected to other people. All of the people I met in the same way, but never got that beer with or did anything that wasn't work-related with. And all the people I wanted to meet for those same reasons, but never actually did. There were a lot of people I followed on social media, that I never met, and might not ever meet now. But some of those people are still in my feed, because they're just here for me to look at.

It's not what it sounds like. A lot of those people are talented photographers, videographers, florists, decorators, artists, and so on... just imagine a list of professions that produce things that are aesthetically pleasing to look at. The end result is that there are people that post things that I like to look at, but they aren't people I'm spending any time with or getting to know. And that feels kind of weird.

One time at an event, I snapped some photos of the musicians playing. I befriended them on Facebook so I could tag them in the photos. One musician, in particular, was a phenomenal singer, in my opinion. Following her on social media was cool because she would post videos of songs she covered or wrote. She is a legitimately exceptional musician who deserves patronage. I don't know anything about her as a person, other than I like hearing her sing. Then, very gradually over time, something undetectable happened. She made fewer and fewer music posts and apparently got really into fitness. Her posts eventually become less like "Check out my song" and more like "Check out my bikini." One day I realized that I couldn't remember the last song she posted. In her defense, creating music isn't nearly as easy to whip together as a selfie, but still. My fingers were crossed for another music video to pop up and wash away the guilt of not hating those bikini photos. Fortunately, she hasn't given up music. I still see occasional music posts from her, mixed into these "aspiring model" photos that weren't previously there. I'm just here to look at you (while I wait for more music).

I remember years ago, trying to promote music that I was making. I remember befriending everyone under the sun that had expressed any interest in local indie music on Twitter and Facebook. I was following hundreds of people I didn't know at all, and all in an attempt to connect with people to get my music into as many ears as possible. And there would be people in those streams that were fairly alluring. Men, women, young, old… I was following everyone. But they were just there in an attempt for me to move records. After the album wasn't new anymore and

I'm Just Here to Look at You.

I gave the promotion stuff a break, I realized I was Facebook friends with hundreds of people I didn't know anything about and my twitter feed was almost completely people I didn't know. I cleaned house. I went through and deleted every person that wasn't "real" to my life. Almost every person. Out of the 300 people that I should have deleted, I deleted about 295. That's because about five people were people I didn't want to not see anymore. If they had asked me why, the answer would be "I'm just here to look at you." And that feels kind of wrong. They lasted for a little while and after some time passed, I realized, "These people are not your friends. You're not going to be friends with them. You don't really want to be friends with them. You just want to look at them. Delete them." And I did.

Everyone looks around at the people around them. You look for signs of danger or signs of safety in people. You seek out familiar faces and you scan for enemies approaching. And while you do all of that, your annoying biology has to go and make you feel terrible every time your genes spot what they think might potentially be an award-winning strand of DNA they could help create. We all get it. We know the rules. Looking is natural.

If you go for a walk at your state fair because you want to look at farm animals, but you can't stop checking out the cabooses on every person you see, that's normal. You're there to see farm animals. It's not like you're at Hooters, pretending the chicken wings brought you there.

People have no problem looking at photos of cute puppies and kitties. We love looking at photos of DIY projects that we will never actually do. We love watching plated foods prepared by famous chefs. We not only enjoy art but are encouraged to stare at it.

There are many different kinds of beauty out there. We can and should appreciate beauty wherever we see it.

What Are You Selling?

"What are you selling" is a reaction gif I wish existed. Something that everyone would universally recognize and find humorous. I wish for this because I think I might use it all the time.

I use the term "selling," not necessarily in reference to a monetary transaction, but rather "pushing" something, someone, an idea, an agenda, whatever. Everyone seems to be pushing something. Sometimes it's obvious. A blatant solicitation of people to buy a product wouldn't require this. Neither would a photo of a guy in the gym taking a selfie of his abs. We know what you're pushing. It's obvious.

Sometimes it's not obvious. Most people don't want to get "pushed" so the pusher has to hide it. They lean on you. They bump into you. They pick you up and set you down somewhere else. Any creative way to push you without you thinking you were pushed. Sometimes, at a glance, I have no idea what is being pushed.

When I started trying to promote my first book (before it was even done) I created an Instagram account, and began following anyone who either had a book in their photos or "checked in" at local bookstores. I collected quite a large number of accounts to follow. And I started to notice a pattern. It's really popular for girls to post pictures of themselves reading books (some guys do it too, but not as many). That's not crazy. Everyone is trying to develop their own personal brand, and we do that in the photos we post publicly. "Look at me doing this thing in this place with these people wearing these clothes." It's normal. It's common with teens trying to define themselves, and slightly less common with older people that aren't trying to win any popularity contests. But normal, all the same.

One account stuck out to me due to the large number of followers. All the photos matched a theme: High quality photography of a girl who likes to read different books in different places. I clicked the

What Are You Selling?

URL in the bio. Her website was straightforward. Paraphrased: "Hi. I'm a girl, I like to read different books, and I read them in different places. Look at my high-quality photos of me doing that on my Instagram account here. Click here to contact me about business opportunities."

It looks like it would be a book review site, but it isn't. There were no reviews I could easily find at first. I eventually found some buried in the site, but they were clearly not the focus. The focus of the site was clearly to direct traffic back to the Instagram account. Could this just be a girl that posed with books, and this was a business of product placement for publishers?

I emailed her.

"Hi. I'm an author. I have a book that will be done at the end of the year. What is it that you do?"

I received no response. If this was a business, I didn't see how anyone could pay her, since she didn't list any goods or services for sale and didn't respond to her emails.

I dove into the posts a little deeper and found where she explained that major publishing companies sent her the books and that she didn't accept submissions from self-publishers. Okay, whatever. But how was she getting paid? Who was paying her? What were they paying her to do? WHAT ARE YOU SELLING?

This isn't the only account like this. There are more than I'd care to count. Similar concepts; usually high-quality photos of books in different places, sometimes with hands turning a page, sometimes a pair of legs crossing the frame, sometimes an entire person. Sometimes the account is mostly on theme with this, but sometimes accounts are a mix of this, plus a selfie from last night's aerobics class. What? WHAT ARE YOU SELLING?

The following is a response to that last question. It's from one of my beta-readers, which I liked so much I am including it:

"My Instagram is kinda like this. But it's definitely a mix of books, and things from my life... I am a complex human being and I like, care about, and think about many things. So, any platform that I might be pushing something on, is going to be an amalgamation of things. So, I guess you could say (speaking strictly for myself) I am pushing my humanity, however complex and seemingly random it may be... I know this probably doesn't help for the book. But you seemed to really want an answer. lol" - Oliver Marie

What Are You Selling?

When my book was done, and I was ready to send ARCs (Advanced Reading Copies) to reviewers, I sent some direct messages to all of these book accounts. Almost no one responded. One person replied with "Ummm... No?"

Now I know they don't answer emails. Most don't answer Instagram DMs. I have this book that I want to get into their hands, but they aren't interested. Fair enough. Time to start unfollowing this stuff. What an epic waste of time.

We're in a new era of wannabe personalities. I'm just as much of an offender, so don't interpret this as a rant against them. I have dabbled in some extremely small doses of a very potent drug called Faux-Fame. Faux-Fame is similar to Celeb-Fame, in that they both involve a one-way knowledge of existence. You know who Tom Cruise is, but he doesn't know who you are. You may like his work, but he isn't familiar with yours. You might be sad if he died, but he couldn't care less if you did. That's the true defining characteristic of the drug Celeb-Fame. However, while Faux-Fame has the exact same negative side effects, it's actually like 99% placebo. Here are some examples:

About 12 years ago I was in a heavy metal band. The only people that came to our shows at tiny corner bars and bought our albums were close friends who felt they owed us support. I was convinced that no one cared. Then two different people from Uruguay messaged me on Facebook to say they were huge fans and that they heard us on the radio there. All of a sudden, I think I'm some world-famous musician, and Milwaukee is just stupid for not noticing me right under its nose.

About 20 years ago I had a cable-access TV show with my buddy Mike Davis. It was called The John & Mike Show and it was on channel 11B on Fridays at 4:30pm. I was pretty sure no one watched it. Then, this one time, after getting the band Korn's autograph at a Best Buy in Greenfield, a teenage girl stopped me to say "Hey, you're John from The John & Mike Show, right?" and I said "Yeah! And I just met Korn! I love Korn!" I ran all the way home staring at my signed CD and a few hours later it dawned on me that a girl tried talking to me about how she watches (or at least knows about) my TV show... And I literally ran away. But I woke up the next day believing I was the next David Letterman.

I'm currently going through a similar feeling with my book. Friends and family have been reading it in what I assume is a show of support. However, I have just begun to see some evidence of strangers reading it of their own legitimate curiosity. I'm probably about to convince myself that I'm a famous author.

With all these examples, it's just the tiniest bit of evidence suggesting that people I've never met know me, and that's all it takes to get the high. And, of course, try to chase it.

I see the appeal of wanting to be an internet personality because (to a tiny degree) I've experienced it from trying to be a podcaster, author, musician, and whatever else. I understand the high you're chasing. I assume it's an easy drug to score from only needing "likes," "shares," and comments to get high.

What I don't get is WHAT ARE YOU SELLING? The podcaster is selling ads. The author is selling books. The musician is selling albums, concerts, and T-shirts.

I've had some time to reflect on my earlier rant about the Instagram people (and this probably applies to all types of people and situations). I think they are probably just working on building their brand as an influencer. It's frustrating to me because on the surface it looks like all they really want is "likes" but you know there is an ulterior motive, such as the financial opportunities that might present itself once they've achieved a high enough level of popularity. Of course, it's too vain to come right out and say "Click 'like' so I can become famous and have a platform to sell something else." Rather, instead we hear some version of "please provide proof of engagement by commenting below with your opinion (that I don't actually care about)."

Thou Shall Not Covet

One time when I was a young kid, there was this toy rifle I really wanted. My mother had taken me birthday-gift shopping for my friend, Joshua. She asked me "What does he want?" I didn't know. "What does he like?" I didn't know. Joshua and I were in Cub Scouts together (the little kid version of Boy Scouts), and we saw each other often because of that. Enough to get invited to his birthday party, but honestly, I had no idea what he was into. My mother gave me a piece of advice that I still use to this day:

"When you don't know what gift to get someone, get them something you would want for yourself." The idea being that if it's something you see value in, then they might too. It's a gamble because not everyone cares about the same things, but it's better than going in totally blind.

Maybe that's common sense. I don't know, because it was given to me at a young age by my infinitely wise mother, so I took it as her gospel. My mother instilled a lot of wisdom on me at that age; Morality based on a biblical foundation but remodeled to fit everyday life. One day it was "It's better to give your friend the toy you want than receive it" (Acts 20:35, Matthew 22:39) and then the next day it was "Stop wanting that toy you just gave your friend." (Exodus 20:17). It was (and still is) a complicated conflict of thoughts to juggle.

Anyway, my mother and I walked up and down the aisles of the toy store, until I saw it. It was a plastic shotgun that would make a loud kazoo-like bang when you cocked it and pulled the trigger. I wanted it REAL bad. And so, that was the gift for Joshua; the toy I could not have for myself. I asked if we could get two, one for him and one for me, but of course the answer was no. It wasn't my birthday, so I didn't deserve it. That's a recurring theme with Christian morality: If you want something, you probably shouldn't want it. If you have something that gives you pleasure, you probably don't deserve it. Flagellant Christians whipped themselves in the 14th-century because they

Thou Shall Not Covet

felt bleeding was required for penance of their sins. Six centuries later, the self-mutilation has been replaced with just feeling ashamed of yourself. But the theme is that "There is nothing I shall want" (Psalm 23) and so wanting anything is something you should feel awful about.

After weeks of not letting up on my inability to not want this toy, my mother made an amendment to Thou Shall Not Covet. The amendment was simple: "You are not allowed to want your friend's toy, but you are allowed to want a toy just like the one your friend has... just not the exact one he owns." Lucky for me, that toy rifle wasn't one of a kind. In an era where almost all toys are mass-produced, coveting one-of-a-kind things was totally avoidable. Unfortunately, there was still the second obstacle: deserving it.

There were two ways I was aware of to deserve a toy: awarded on Christmas and birthdays for year-long good behavior and by suffering through chores to earn the money to buy it. Yes, I believed the purpose of work was to suffer; a penance for the sin of greed. Perhaps I was too young to understand the economics, but that was my takeaway at the time. Adults weren't actually trading money to their kids in exchange for a valuable service kids offered; they were trying to teach kids a lesson. It should have been a lesson about the economics of trade, but I took it as a lesson about how you have to suffer to get things you want.

The math was simple: I made $1 per week for my allowance. The plastic toy gun was $16. On good behavior alone, it made more sense to wait four months for Christmas than to save for four months and spend four months of salary. Plus, I didn't want to wait four months. I wanted it NOW. That's extra sinful, so I would have to figure out a way to be really unhappy to speed up the process. Raking leaves, doing dishes, whatever it took to be miserable enough to deserve that toy gun.

As an 8-year-old, my ADHD was as bad or worse than it is nowadays. One symptom is hyper-focusing, which is an inability to focus on anything else, because one thing takes up all of my attention. The one thing I hyper-focus on is usually something of low priority, so I neglect things I should be focused on because I can't stop focusing on something less important. In this story, I was pretty hyper-focused on that toy gun. So much so, that I would talk about it with complete strangers. Someone saying, "How are you?" prompted me to reply with the specifics of my dire situation "There is this toy gun I really want, but it costs $16 and I only get $1 a week allowance." I wasn't asking for anything. I was simply describing my predicament.

Thou Shall Not Covet

At this time in my life, my dad was in the church choir. A handsome-voiced baritone, he sang with the basses in the choir loft. So as not to be separated from him, my mother and I would sit in the balcony pew next to the choir. It was a great view, with a front-row-like music experience. But the one downside was that it was the longest trip to the bathroom. You had to walk down the steps and then all the way up to the front of the church, and the bathrooms were located behind the sacristy. It was quite the journey, so being gone for several minutes made sense. One time in particular, I encountered a man at the bottom of the steps in the lobby. He likely greeted me with something like "How are you?" and from the previous paragraph, you already know my answer.

A generous man, he simply reached into his pocket, pulled out a twenty-dollar bill, and said something along the lines of "Do something gracious like this for someone else, someday." I'm sure I thanked him, and I went to the bathroom, then back up to my pew for the rest of mass. After mass, when I was allowed to speak, I told my mother the good news. She was not jubilant for me, the way I thought she would be. She took the twenty dollars and walked over and told my father. They both looked concerned. They had me point out who did it, and my dad returned the money to him. I still remember some of the things he said to my dad: "I give money away all the time. I give money to charities and it makes me happy." I remember my dad saying "He's not a charity. Please take the money back."

I had no idea what happened. What did I do wrong? What did that guy do wrong? I was a kid that wanted a toy that I couldn't afford. This was a guy that liked giving money to strangers because he liked how it made him feel. Win-win, right? No. The problem, I concluded, was that I didn't deserve to be happy without being unhappy first. Getting what you want without suffering for it wasn't an option. Better that this man give his money to a charity where people are already suffering. I wasn't suffering, so I wasn't a charity. I wasn't suffering, so I didn't deserve anything. To earn it, was to suffer.

I metaphorically whipped my flesh with the most unpleasant chores. Chores that didn't bring any value to my parents. My leaf-raking sucked... leaves everywhere. My dishwashing sucked... parents just re-washed them when I was done. You get the picture. I suffered, I got the money, and I bought that toy gun. And it was a lot of fun for a least a couple days.

I learned that if you succeed at wanting nothing, then you don't have to suffer for anything. But more importantly, I learned a behavior that I still practice to this day; I turn away things. I turn away compliments and praise. I feel shame for things I have that I didn't suffer to get. I can't logically justify it. It's just something I experienced a long time ago, and now I'm trying to decide if it's something I should try to unlearn.

There are a few memories I have that conflict with the memory above. For example, I remember that after my Great Uncle Zig died, my father would help my Great Aunt Irene with things, such as driving her to the grocery store. I would come along and help grab items off the lower shelves and carry groceries to the car and into the house. One time I noticed her slip my dad a twenty-dollar bill. I asked him about it on the car ride home, and he explained his position: The right thing to do was to help Aunt Irene, because she needed help and she was family and we love her. It is also okay to accept money in exchange for the service he was providing her. I just couldn't wrap my head around this. How could it be both things? Is it a charity, or is it a business? How can you help someone and also accept payment? I determined that events had to happen in a specific order for this to work.

First, either someone would need to ask for help, or you would have to offer help. I feel like this detail matters, but I never picked up on which means what. Anyway, after that, you then offer the help without any financial agreement. They ask, you give. That's the charity. Now, it's up to the person to decide if they want to offer money. Maybe offering money makes them feel better, because they don't want to see themselves as a charity. This delicate dance occurs where one person offers services as a charity, and then the other person decides to turn it into a transaction instead of a gift. Or maybe they look at it as an exchange of gifts. They both feel positive by giving each other something. One gives a service, the other gives money.

I get it... I think. But then isn't every business transaction on par with a gift exchange? The difference I guess is that with business, there is an agreed upon service or product and an agreed upon compensation. When you do it without discussing a price tag, then it's an exchange of gifts... I think. I don't know, this feels like a really thin line.

I feel like deep down, there must have been a conflict of thoughts in my dad's head. I believe he felt a duty to help his aunt. I believe he wanted to be helpful and spend time with her. I believe he had 100% honorable intentions. I also believe that he likely got the phone call from her at the last minute, and probably had other things planned to do with his time. He helped her as something he wanted to do, and he felt he was providing an act of charity, while also likely feeling he was "suffering" a loss of his time. It's not selfish. I think you can simultaneously enjoy your time with someone and doing a good deed while also mourning the loss of the time you wanted to keep for yourself. If all he wanted to do was spend time with her and help her, and he didn't want to do anything else, then he likely would have turned that money away. He wouldn't be able to accept money for not "suffering" to some degree. Why would he accept money for something that he enjoyed doing? He must have, to some tiny degree, not enjoyed some aspect of it.

Another motivation for dad to accept Aunt Irene's money was because of her pride. Besides the fact that paying him most likely made her happy, she also probably wouldn't have asked for his help again if he had turned down payment.

Fast forward almost 30 years. I was recently enjoying reading the Wikipedia pages on different ancient Greek philosophies. Specifically, Epicureanism. It was refreshing to read thoughts on ethics, completely independent of the Bible.

Epicurus believed that "pleasure" is the greatest thing in life, which is a type of Hedonism. Hedonism is sometimes vague and doesn't necessarily always have a game plan, whereas Epicureanism goes on to better define different pleasures and how to go about pursuing them. For example, one should limit the things they want, live modestly, and pursue knowledge. A goal is to reach a state of tranquility where one is without fear or pain, therein defining a broader concept of pleasure.

I can already tell that I'm a lot more interested in this than Bible quotes. I've only just begun to research it, but so far I've seen a common occurrence. It's best to limit the material things you want. It's best to avoid suffering. If you must suffer a small amount, it should be in order to receive a larger amount of pleasure.

I'm sure there are aspects of Epicureanism that I don't agree with. There is no single source for all the answers in life (besides Google). But different types of philosophy is something I should probably research more.

Skunks

I often wonder what life for the skunk would have been like, had it not had the stinky gland thing going on. If you or your pet has ever been sprayed by a skunk, then the sight of a skunk brings paralyzing fear. Where would the skunk be today, had it not smelled like such a jerk?

Let me start off by catching up anyone on skunk spray who hasn't dealt with it up close and personally. It doesn't count if you've smelled it off in the distance. Skunk spray is to the smelling senses what I'd imagine hell-made salsa is to taste. In hell I don't think salsa is super-hot. If you're going to be tortured with super-

UNCREDIBLE THOUGHTS

hot salsa, demons might just as well jam hot coals in your mouth. No, salsa in hell is just a normal hot salsa, but it never goes away. It lingers for eternity and you never get used to it. That is what skunk spray is. It's appalling, but it wouldn't be SO HORRID if it just went away. Skunk smell does go away, eventually. My dog got sprayed, tried to wipe it off on my carpet, and my house was thereon haunted with an odor that lasted over 2 years. The smell was like an airborne virus. Any air that touched the affected area was then infected air. Anything that air touched became a new affected area. Example: Our clothes in a different room all smelled like skunk because the air in the infected area went into our cold-air-return, through the furnace, and up through all the vents into every room in the house. When I left the house and went to my office downtown the next day, my clothes made the whole office smell like skunk.

I actually think it's more of a psychological agony than just an atrocious smell. The inability to control it and the fear that other people will smell it, to me, was worse than the actual smell. After several treatments of both homemade recipes and store-bought skunk deodorizer, we could still smell it. Anytime I caught a whiff, it would remind me of my lack of control, and it fed my paranoias. After a year or so it was gone for the dry months, but humidity always "woke it up." After 2+ years, it was finally completely gone.

Skunks

Have you seen a skunk up close? If you can get past the paralyzing fear, you'll notice that they are adorable. They look like the halfway point between a cat and stuffed teddy bear. They are omnivores but are relatively chill. They can't see things that are far away, so something really needs to get close for it to spray. The skunk's only line of defense is to spray that nasty stuff from its ass-glands. It's safe to say that the skunk as we know it wouldn't exist at all without that foul odor. And before you say "good," think about what would be in its place. What we have now is a bashful animal that smells so gross that most predators won't eat it. I'm guessing they would have evolved much differently if they were getting picked off constantly. They'd probably be more aggressive. They'd have to develop a different line of defense and might have learned to attack by biting. They might have developed the ability to see farther, run faster, and perhaps even attack offensively instead of just defensively. Well, we don't want that. The very thing we hate about the skunk is also the same thing that prevents it from being an even bigger asshole.

I think the most logical future for skunks is that of domesticated eugenics. Let's face it, if they didn't stink, they'd probably be better cats than cats are. If you can domesticate cats, you can domesticate skunks. We'd just have to somehow crossbreed them to not have the anal gland thing. Or to have it, but not use it. My dog, Cassette, has anal glands that stink sometimes and need to get drained, but she doesn't spray them at will. But anal gland smells are her worst feature. She's a great dog except for her stinky ass, which she can't help.

Love, fear, and respect the skunk in its current form. It's not the perfect animal, but nobody is perfect. And we shouldn't grade animals based on their ability to co-exist with us. If you see a skunk, bow your head in respect and back away.

White History Month Shouldn't Exist

I can't be the only one who thought of this. In fact, I'm sure a quick Google search would show me enough evidence for how unoriginal this thought is that it would discourage me from writing this chapter. However, I don't want to be discouraged, and so I won't Google it. Anyway, here is that thought:

Isn't it painfully obvious that the celebration of multiple European cultures is in itself exactly what people are asking for when they say, "Why isn't there a White History Month?"

First of all, there is a difference between people advocating for White Pride verses White Power. White Power is the most backwards-thinking insanity that any human could cling to. Should white communities and cultures have "power" over non-whites? No. Shut up. Just shut your stupid mouth. You're making the rest of us look bad. White Pride, on the other hand, while still dumb, is more understandable. White people want a culture and a community to be a part of just as much as anyone else. The problem is "white" isn't a culture or a community.

I live in Milwaukee, the city that hosts the world's largest music festival every single summer. It is called Summerfest, and it is such a big deal that it requires a huge chunk of lakeside county property adorned with amphitheaters and restaurant facilities. And while Summerfest is filled to the brim for just under 2 weeks a year, that property attempts to make itself useful for multiple small fests throughout the rest of the year. Some of those fests include…

- Polish Fest
- German Fest
- Irish Fest
- Festa Italiana
- Mexican Fiesta

- Pridefest
- A ton of charity walks/runs
- and much more.

To summarize all of the festivals: we Milwaukeeans love any excuse to pay way too much for a beer while standing outside. And in a strange way, our extremely segregated city has this uplifting way of coming together for a blending of the cultures to share in our mutual alcoholism and love for ethnic food.

We essentially throw several "White Pride" festivals every single year, and no one gets upset about it. Saying "White Pride" obviously wouldn't go over too well, but call it "Irish Fest" and it's fine. And I think that says something important about celebrating heritage and culture in an INCLUSIVE way. It says "I'm proud of who I am and where I come from, yada yada yada… but seriously, everyone, you need to try these pierogies."

So why the pushback on something like Black History Month? When you say "Why isn't there a White History Month?" I can't help but wonder if your invitation was lost in the mail or something. Yes, you and everyone else are invited to Black History Month, just like everyone is invited to Pridefest.

UNCREDIBLE THOUGHTS

You don't have to be LGBTQ+ to go to Pridefest. No matter who you are, you can drink overpriced beer and watch bands play in the sun alongside the proud LGBTQ+ community. And if you're an ally, you can be proud of that.

I feel like that SHOULD be the way non-blacks feel about Black History Month. We're invited to come to the party, learn, share, appreciate, reflect, and whatever else. Hell, even taking baby steps like reciting "Chuck Berry helped pave the way for modern rock music" is a step in the right direction.

In the other eleven months of the year, everyone can celebrate St. Patrick's Day, Oktoberfest, Bastille Day, Fat Tuesday, and any endless number of moments from European history.

But honestly, "White Pride" is ridiculous when we know about all the subcategories. We have no reason to unite under the umbrella of pigment, because we often have a good idea about our heritage. We have the privilege of culturally identifying with something dorky like polka, step dance, gelato, or lederhosen.

It's a different story for many black Americans whose ancestors were born into slavery, knowing nothing about their heritage. It makes sense that they celebrate their color, and not unknown family history.

Okay, I'll wrap this up. Here is the "too long; didn't read" version of this chapter:

"White Pride" is stupid, because there isn't white cultural identity. Stop saying there should be a white history month when we celebrate European history year round.

Your Unhappiness Is Stupid; Time For A Nap

I need a nap, but not because I think I feel tired, necessarily. I need a nap the way my cranky toddler needs a nap when she's upset that she doesn't want to sit down or stand up. When she can't stop crying because she can't watch two different TVs in two different rooms at the same time. My antidote for these situations is simply "When your unhappiness is stupid, it's time for a nap." I notice these childlike temper tantrums brewing in my own mind all the time.

I get upset while doing chores, but I also get upset when I don't do them.

UNCREDIBLE THOUGHTS

I get upset that I have to make time to go to the gym. I get upset that I'm at the gym and not somewhere else sitting down. I get upset that I'm sweating. Or if I don't do any of that, I get upset that I didn't work out like I should.

I get upset because I ate all the Doritos. I get upset that Doritos make me fat. I get upset that I love Doritos. I get upset because I forgot to buy more Doritos.

I get upset that super rich people are so rich. I get upset that I'm not rich.

I get upset that some people are intolerant. I get upset that it feels hypocritical that I am intolerant of intolerant people.

I get upset that there are no rooms in the house I want to be in. I get upset that I can't choose what to watch on TV. I get upset that I'm acting like a toddler.

It's time for a nap.

Assholes, And The Rest

My whole life I've had an uncontrollable urge to lump humans into two categories. For the longest time, those two categories were Assholes and Not Assholes. However, as I've matured I've realized that many factors are opinions and perceptions. Things I currently believe to be true are always at risk of compromise when proven wrong or when new information presents itself. I end up thinking "I think I know how the world is and I know how it should be, but I could also have no idea and/or be completely wrong." It ends up being hard to place all of mankind into two categories as subjective as Assholes and Not

Assholes when you fully acknowledge that no one person gets to judge. Sure, each individual person could sort through the population in this way (all with different conclusions), but that just brings us back to the drawing board.

Why do I have this urge to simplify people? I'm pretty sure it's because judging people is incredibly exhausting. And let's face it; we judge people all the time. When we do it at the primal level we try to assess if someone is a threat to us. That means we need to do it fast. We need to observe as much about the subject as we can, cross-reference that to information we already have, and do that in the shortest amount of time possible. Our brains do this automatically to avoid being murdered, so you can't really be upset about that. But beyond the primal instincts, judging people to understand their character really requires a lot of work and the only way you can do it without being a jerk is to put the work in.

I think this is why we generally associate "being judgey" as a negative characteristic. Specifically that most of the time most people are lazy judges. The more time and effort you put into understanding another person's perspective, the more understandable their mindset and actions will be. I mean, what's negative about that? Nothing. That's why I think when we say someone is "judgey," what that really means is that they judge lazily.

If everyone had an infinite amount of time, energy, and the desire to do so, we could all come to a universal truth about morality and how to classify everyone's character. In this impossible situation, very few people would likely fall into the asshole category, because there would be a handicap of understanding on every person. It would be like a giant game of golf where almost everyone ties for 1st place, because truly understanding who they are would apply an empathy handicap.

And so it would seem like I already know that I can't lump people into categories like this. And yet, I still feel the lazy primal judgey urge to do it. My newest thought is that I need to reframe the sorting process. If it lands on me to judge the subject's actions, I could be observing them incorrectly. If it lands on me to judge my own interpretation of their actions, that seems like it could be a truer verdict. It's really more about deciding how I see people, not deciding who people (that I don't truly know) really are.

I feel obliged to tell the story of why I came up with my new system.

I pulled up to the gas station pump. In the spot in front of me was another car. While I pumped my gas,

I saw the driver and the passenger walk out of the building and get in their car. They closed the car doors and started the car. A few seconds passed before they reopened their car doors, tossed out piles of garbage onto the ground, and then drove away. I stood there in shock. They threw garbage on the ground literally only a few feet away from a garbage can. I kept thinking about it over and over. Was this laziness? I mean, it was, but was it malicious laziness? Or was it simply stupidity? Did they think "Once the garbage is out of the car, it's gone forever from everywhere" the way an idiot would? Did they think "Ha ha! Now the gas station employee has to clean up after us!" like a person who is a complete shit-bag? Maybe they never thought at all about the consequences of their actions.

That lead to my newest categories. Yes, I've tossed out Assholes and Not Assholes, and I've replaced them with this over-worded complicated grading scale:

1. Those that display NO awareness for how their actions affect others.
2. Those that display an awareness for how their actions affect others BUT DO NOT observably care.
3. Those that display a SEMI-awareness for how their actions affect others AND they observably try to maximize the positive BUT fail to minimize their negative effect on others.

4. Those that display an awareness for how their actions affect others AND they observably try to minimize negative effects on others.
5. Those that display an awareness of how their actions affect others AND they observably try to minimize negative effects AS WELL AS maximize positive effects on others.

Here is the twist. It's not your typical 1-5 scale where 1 sucks and 5 is awesome. I actually think 2 is far worse than 1. All humans are ignorant about most things. While ignorance is not a virtue, it isn't "wrong" to not know something, because the solution is to learn it. And if your only problem is that you have no idea that you are making other people's lives worse, than you can learn that, and correct it. However, if you do learn it, and choose not to correct it, then you have moved on to #2, which is clearly in the "asshole" category.

I'll even go as far to say that we shouldn't expect everyone to be a #5, either. Simply because what you THINK is positively affecting one person or group might actually be negatively affecting a different person or group. And so an attempt at #5 might actually land you at #3.

No, where we should all be, and also expect from each other, is #4.

I think what I was trying to do with the 2-group sorting system of Assholes and Not Assholes, was basically saying "Are you a 2 or a 4?" But that didn't take into account ignorance, intentions, and most importantly how I observe them. A #1 could mean the subject is ignorant to their effects on others, but a #1 could also mean that I AM NOT OBSERVANT enough to detect how subtle the subject's actions are. It really puts it back on me. It's not "What kind of person is this?" but rather "How well am I seeing who they really are?"

While the result was the same regardless of intentions and perceptions, I decided that it was important for my own quality of life to assume they were dumbasses. Because ignorance is solvable. They can learn, and go on to correct their behaviors going forward. That's a much more positive and uplifting perspective for me to have. That's a society I want to be a part of: a bunch of dummies learning how to be admirable citizens (myself included). The alternative is a real bummer; the idea that they aren't stupid, but rather just terrible people. People who know better, only care about themselves, and choose the attitude of "fuck everyone else."

Who was the most affected by my experience with the litterers? I was. I was the one who picked up their garbage. I thought about it all night to the point of reformulating my entire internal measuring system for grading human morality. It haunts me to this day to imagine a society where no one cares about anyone other than themselves. That was why I thought it was so important to put the burden on myself. I can't know everyone's intentions. I can't understand their entire life's story leading up to their decisions I observe. I judge what I'm seeing, but that judgement is on me. The only person that judgement affects is me.

Do I Have A Mild Case Of Hoarding?

The following is from a blog entry I wrote in May of 2017, one year and seven months before the show "Tidying Up with Marie Kondo" became extremely popular on Netflix. I feel required to share that so you don't think I'm just ripping off overused memes.

When I watch those reality TV shows that showcase examples of extreme hoarding, it always makes me feel better about myself. However, justifying my own behavior by simply comparing it to more extreme behavior doesn't mean I don't have a problem. The same way the show "My 600-Pound Life" doesn't make me healthy, watching extreme hoarding shows doesn't make me a minimalist.

Now, I ADMIRE minimalism. I really do. And watching examples of minimalism has the opposite effect on me that watching a hoarding show does. I see examples of minimalism and then I feel really bad about myself. I suppose if I were to tell myself to "not feel bad" after watching a show about minimalism, great health, or other admirable behaviors, then it would only be fair to tell myself "But don't forget that you SHOULD still feel bad" after watching their opposites.

But behaviors like hoarding seem to only be a problem when the negative effects are visible to others. When a house is overflowing with stuff and there are no floor or surface areas left, that's when we say "DAMN! THAT'S MESSED UP!" However, we don't say anything in the early stages. I often think about how organization is kind of a way of enabling hoarding. For example, a giant stack of old bills and receipts stacked on top of the microwave makes a viewer say "Why don't you just throw those out?" However, put them in files and sort those into a filing cabinet, and suddenly that's responsible behavior. We don't ask to see the dates on those bills, because they look like they are where they belong. The same thing goes for clutter. Does it make it okay to have stuff you don't

Do I Have A Mild Case Of Hoarding?

need by organizing it into boxes, labeling those boxes, and then stacking them neatly on shelves in your basement?

That's what makes me think the perception is about space, not behavior. If you walked into an immaculately clean home, you might not think there is anything wrong. What you don't see is that the owners of that home might have 3 storage units full of stuff they "cleaned" out of their house. Without the storage units, the same amount of stuff might have looked concerning in that home.

And what's up with collections? Where is the line in the sand between collecting things and hoarding? That again seems to fall into the realm of perception. For example, I've never seen any guitarists looked at negatively for having 12 guitars, even though you can only play one at a time. A home library with a large collection of books is considered elegant, but without the shelves, a stack of boxes filled with books makes you ask "Why don't you just drop those off at Goodwill?" It would seem the organization of "stuff" absolves it from being clutter, even though it's the same behavior.

So am I a hoarder because I own things that don't constantly bring me joy or function? Would the answer be "no" if I move into a larger home? Would the answer be "yes" if I moved into a smaller home?

I don't think I'm a hoarder as much as I'm overwhelmed about cleaning. And by cleaning I mean actually getting rid of things, not just moving things around. I am very capable of parting with possessions... I'm just too lazy and overwhelmed to do it.

My mother suggested I add something that explained that she is trying to cure herself of her own hoarding habits. I'll just quote her notes instead:

"You can mention that your mother is trying to get over hoarding by giving you 'stuff.' Stuff she doesn't use and you probably won't use either. '...but it was your grandmother's.' etc." - Donna Marszalkowski

I highly recommend having your mother proofread your writing. Mothers have been practicing their whole lives at criticizing their children's choices. Finally, there is a context for which this is useful.

Cassettes

It was 1994 when I first heard Soundgarden's Black Hole Sun on the radio. The radio was the main way to consume new music then. There was MTV, but not everyone had cable. I sure didn't. Plus MTV was kind of a Top 40 sort of thing, while radio stations were a little more genre focused.

Anyway, I was 12 years old. I played the alto saxophone in middle school band, and my favorite cassette tape at that moment was probably Paula Abdul's "Spellbound." I was 113 pounds. Just trying to paint a picture, here.

UNCREDIBLE THOUGHTS

So I heard Black Hole Sun on the radio and I fell in love with it. It was my favorite song, even if I wasn't sure why. Up to that point in my life, I didn't necessarily care about most rock music.

I remember listening to the radio constantly, with my fingers crossed that Black Hole Sun would come on during the same window of time that I could listen. Maybe it was my short attention span or maybe radio didn't play the same 5 hits on a loop back then, but I wasn't getting enough of it.

I did the only thing a 12-year-old with no money could do: I broke the law.

Using my dual-cassette tape recorder, I would record the radio in 90 minute blocks onto tapes, and then from those, dub individual songs I liked onto a second tape. Between the radio's initial heavy compression and the quality loss from tape-dubbing, it's hard to believe what I was doing was illegal. The finished product in no way resembled the quality of a store-bought album.

I had a similar process for obtaining videos of songs. I didn't have cable, so there was no MTV in my life. I would check the newspaper in the TV section to see who the musical guests would be on Leno, Letterman, and SNL. If it was a band I liked or had heard was "cool" I would load a VHS tape into the recorder, watch the whole show (that I didn't care about), and then record the song in the last 3 minutes of the show. SNL was different. It wasn't at the very end. There were 2 whole songs, but I was never exactly sure when they would come on, so I'd have to stay on my toes to hit record and get those in their entirety. From the looks of YouTube nowadays, I'm not the only one who did that.

I was just reflecting on that and how much has changed in the last 20-some years, as I watch any video I want to watch, instantly on YouTube. Or how I can stream pretty much any album I want to hear instantly. It's really impressive. But I often wonder what it's like for younger people who can now get any digital content they want instantly. Are there any positive effects that come from a childhood which lacked instant gratification? I don't know. That question opens the door to others, such as:

- Was there any benefit to needing to physically go to the library to learn something?
- Was there any benefit that came from being pretty much completely off the grid whenever you weren't within hearing-range of your kitchen phone?

I have a feeling that there wasn't. I think things were just harder and yielded worse results. Has instant gratification desensitised this generation to the joys of delayed gratification? Possibly.

Kids today are really damn smart. They build robots and write code and use the same software for fun that adults use at their jobs. All without adults helping them. They teach themselves with the help of YouTube videos. The bar of what is "great" has been raised SO HIGH with YouTube. That also kind of seems like a negative for them.

Back when I was a teen, if you were mediocre at something, then you were kind of great at it. It's like there were only two categories: Bad and Not Bad. A quick YouTube search will now show you that there are tons of people who can do your favorite thing better than you can. We all know that "there is always someone out there who is better," but only now is it so easily confirmed. Advancements in technology seem to have made young people more talented (relative to the same age 20 years ago), but are confidence levels the same? Does a kid, who is above-average at something, look to the internet and conclude they must not be above average, since so many people online are so much better than they are?

Cassettes

I guess I'm trying to say that I both envy the resources kids have today growing up that I didn't, but I'm also grateful that the bar was set slightly lower for me.

That One Time I Peed My Pants

When I was in 1st grade, I peed my pants in the middle of class. I don't remember it that well (I was only 6 years old). I remember my mom picking me up and taking me home early that day. At the time I thought, "Wow, I sure am lucky Mom needed me to come home early, today of all days."

REGARDLESS, one of two things must have happened:

- My peers realized this was an embarrassing accident and never mentioned it ever again. You know, because 6-year-olds are super polite and always think about others and never tease each other.

...or...

- My teacher did some **ninja shit** to make sure the other kids in class didn't notice, while getting me out of there.

I'd like to also note that I thought I "got away with it." Mom played it off like I must have sat in something wet. My teacher never acknowledged it to me.

It might be 31 years too late, but thank you Mrs. Moody and Mom for saving me from permanent embarrassment-induced psychological damage.

Tweets I've Tweeted on Twitter

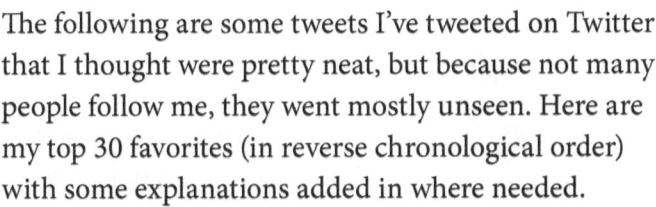

The following are some tweets I've tweeted on Twitter that I thought were pretty neat, but because not many people follow me, they went mostly unseen. Here are my top 30 favorites (in reverse chronological order) with some explanations added in where needed.

- 🐦 "This salsa is kind of spicy. What will put out this fire on my tongue? Oh look, cold wet salsa!"

- 🐦 I'm not afraid of being dead and I really enjoy feeling alive. But to be honest, I'm fucking terrified of being anywhere in-between.

UNCREDIBLE THOUGHTS

> 🐦 It's easier to make all your dreams come true if you barely have any. #epicureanism

Epicurus, an ancient Greek philosopher, taught his students to try to let go of their love of material possessions, because if the pursuit of "stuff" is what they expected would bring them pleasure, they would never have enough. Almost contradictory, he then suggested trying to limit their goals in life to things like the pursuit of knowledge and friendships. But on the surface, it makes sense to me: If you never wanted it, you don't regret not having it. Want less; sounds good in theory. Probably much harder in practice.

> 🐦 I want to hang a poster in my garage of @AOC ...wearing her usual professional attire. Maybe it can have an inspiring quote at the bottom. Actually, replace "garage" with "daughter's room."

The jury is still out on if I'm in love with Alexandria Ocasio-Cortez's politics. She has said a lot of things I've liked, and she's said things that made me roll my eyes. But overall, I like her confidence and intelligence. The elephant in the room is that she is young and beautiful, which is why I thought I'd joke about a poster in a garage. She's lovely enough to ogle, but in reality, it makes more sense to look up to her as a representative for Americans and a role model for girls interested in politics. No matter how you look at it, she's a model.

- I'm not impressed by orchestra conductors. There, I said it.

- If only one out of a million people like what you're making, that's over seventy-thousand people.

- "...And the only reason for being a bee is to make honey." - Winnie the Pooh ...Wait. By that logic, what is the only reason for being a human? I'm terrified to know. Or maybe I need to listen to philosophical advice from someone who isn't a cartoon bear. #dadlife

- I live closer to Russia than to Hawaii. #mindblown

- "I'm really thirsty. I guess I'll eat Doritos until I feel sick." #whybrain? #why?

- I'm thankful for more things than I can list or prioritize. Life is good. If your life isn't, let me know how I can help. Happy Thanksgiving.

- Please reconsider wearing pajamas in public. Please.

UNCREDIBLE THOUGHTS

- I think as far as rodents go, Felicity Jones is probably the most attractive.

- I've never seen a Peppa Pig episode I didn't like. But I want to murder all these adults on YouTube who play with toys. Maybe it's time to turn the TV off. #dadlife

- I just spilled coffee ALL OVER myself in my car. Shirt and pants soaked. I'm about to walk into @Target anyways. Why did I laugh? The last time I spilled something on myself I was upset for an entire year.

- To the woman who was holding her infant on her lap in the moving car next to me: Yes, I was judging you. I was also deciding if this is the type of thing I'm supposed to call the cops over or not.

- Alright, Earth... We build a giant tube on the moon that hangs all the way down into earth's atmosphere. Then the freezing cold space air can pour down into our atmosphere and air-condition the world! Global Warming solved! #IFAILEDHIGHSCHOOLFRESHMANSCIENCE

- I like maritime/nautically-themed environments... but I don't care much for deep water, the bugs that hang around docks, or hot weather without access to air conditioning. I think I just really like kitschy seafood restaurants.

> #Statistics #question: I made a survey. So far, 30% of the takers chose option A, 40% chose B, and 30% chose C. So, most people chose B... but not really, because most people chose NOT B. Wait. So most people prefer B and most people also don't? I think my brain's OS crashed.

This is also why I kind of fear the idea of multi-party politics gaining popularity over the two-party system that everyone seems to hate. The winner could potentially not represent the majority.

> 1993: A Jehovah's Witness didn't stand for the pledge of allegiance in my class. I learned our flag represents the freedom to not worship it.

This is my response to the way-too-big-a-deal made about kneeling for the national anthem at sporting events. If an 11-year-old version of me could wrap my head around the actual freedom the flag represents, then so should grownups.

> I want to join a secret society, but no one will tell me where the meetings are held. #dadjokes #butseriously

UNCREDIBLE THOUGHTS

I looked into Freemasons, Elks, Mooses, and the Rotary Club. None of them are what I'm looking for. I think what I want is to join the Illuminati. But since I just talked about them in a published book, I probably blew my chances of joining.

- 🐦 Watching the drill sergeant scream complements in Forrest Gump's face brings me irrational happiness.

- 🐦 My daughter just pooped herself... but I think she's still going... so I guess I'll just wait this out.

- 🐦 There is nothing my daughter would rather drool on and into more than my iPhone's charging port.

- 🐦 Mics are tools for pro vocalists.
  Amateurs also use them to sing.
  Does anyone enjoy using pickaxes?
  Are "amateur coal miners" a thing?

A poem I wrote about the over-saturation of enjoyable professions.

- 🐦 The tuba is the fart joke of the music world.

- 🐦 I'm dreaming of a white Christmas.
  Snow, that is... not in a supremacist kind of way.

Tweets I've Tweeted on Twitter

> 🐦 They say money can't buy happiness, but I imagine poverty can cause depression.

> 🐦 I'm going to be a father!!!

Just a reminder that this list is ordered chronologically, not by importance. Otherwise, "I'm going to be a father!!!" would be #1.

> 🐦 The only people who should complain about the weather are those working outside. And people with long commutes. So everyone, I guess.

> 🐦 I have a Romeo & Juliet relationship with peanut butter. We love one another, but the peanut family wants to kill my family. #Allergies

My mother and nephew are very allergic to peanuts. While I love peanut butter, getting to eat it as a child was always rare since it wasn't allowed in the house.

Feel free to follow me on Twitter. My username is @JohnnyMarsz. Unlike the kinds of accounts that I mentioned in my chapter "What Are You Selling?" you'll noticed my twitter account is a blatant solicitation to sell you my books by sharing tiny bits of my thoughts that evolve into my published essays.

Everyone Is A Feminist Until Proven Jerks

I've made it a point to vocalize that I assume everyone is a feminist until they say something misogynistic. What I mean is simply that I assume that everyone thinks men and women are equally human and entitled to the same human rights, unless they say something contrary. Shouldn't we all just assume that people aren't sexist until they prove they are sexist? I like to imagine that the vast majority of us are working toward a society that treats men and women fairly. Sure, we know that some people aren't helping that cause, but I want to assume that almost everyone is on our side. Innocent until proven guilty, right?

Well, first we have to look at how feminism is being defined to know the parameters of who is on this team.

---

fem·i·nism (noun)

Merriam-Webster

1. the theory of the political, economic, and social equality of the sexes
2. organized activity on behalf of women's rights and interests

Cambridge Academic Content Dictionary

1. an organized effort to give women the same economic, social, and political rights as men
2. the belief that women should be allowed the same rights, power, and opportunities as men and be treated in the same way, or the set of activities intended to achieve this state

Oxford University Dictionaries

1. The advocacy of women's rights on the ground of the equality of the sexes.

Encyclopædia Britannica

1. the belief in social, economic, and political equality of the sexes.

Everyone Is A Feminist Until Proven Jerks

You get the idea. It's all about equality, not superiority. And yet people are really cautious about throwing the title around. A lot of women (and especially men) are afraid to identify as a feminist. But why would anyone be afraid of identifying as someone who supports equality?

I think the "response" to feminism is the problem. This idea that a claim like "Women should have the right to vote," somehow required a rebuttal. Somewhere in this mess of interpreting the meaning of feminism (which is clearly defined in multiple dictionaries), people feel the need to be defensive. As if to say that feminism is somehow shouting in their face, and so they need to shout back.

If we look at Cambridge's second definition of feminism, we see the wording "...women should be **allowed** the same rights, power, and opportunities as men..." That definition might bring up a whole different debate about whether our society is or isn't a patriarchy.

My argument in defense of feminism semantics is that we can define feminism long before we ever get to the patriarchy debate. Here, enjoy this "choose your own adventure" list I made:

1. What is your gender? Regardless of your answer, proceed to #2, because it doesn't matter.
2. Do you think men and women should have the same rights? If yes, go to #3. If no, go to #6.
3. **Congratulations, you are a feminist.** Next question: Do you think that in our society it is men, and not women, who are in control of who is allowed rights, power, and opportunities? If Yes, go to #4. If no, go to #5.
4. **You are still a feminist.** You believe you must defeat the patriarchy's oppression of women's rights. [END]
5. **You are still a feminist.** You believe you must defeat the ignorant to spread the gospel of equality. [END]
6. **You're not a feminist.** You are either ignorant or oppressive. The good news is that it isn't too late to change. [START OVER]

The question of "do we live in a patriarchy" does not need to be answered in order to establish if you are a feminist or not.

I think the next defensive response that arises when trying to define feminism is that "Equality is not equity." It seems like equality was too big of a concept for some people to wrap their heads around. Once again, a vague idea about making life fair for everyone sparks a defensive response in some people. The "life isn't fair" reflex kicks in for them. But again, this debate can occur long after establishing if you are or are not a feminist. That's because we aren't really debating the definition of equality. The debate is about the value of equality, not what equality is.

---

equal·i·ty (noun)

Merriam-Webster

1. the quality or state of being equal

Cambridge Academic Content Dictionary

1. the right of different groups of people to receive the same treatment

Oxford University Dictionaries

1. The state of being equal, especially in status, rights, or opportunities.

Encyclopædia Britannica

1. Generally, an ideal of uniformity in treatment or status by those in a position to affect either.

What is the next rebuttal? That the sexes are not equal? Well, only one of those feminism definitions made reference to equality of the sexes without obvious context of it being political, economic, and social equality. The other five clearly mean men and women should have political, economic, and social equality. None are saying men and women are exactly the same. But like before, if the equality of the sexes requires debate, it can occur after you've determined you are or are not a feminist.

And I think this goes without saying, but if someone says or does something stupid in the name of feminism, that doesn't speak for all feminists, right? You can search the internet and find idiots making absolutely any group look inferior. But I wouldn't encourage it. If you want to believe an entire group is wrong, it's not hard to find examples to validate your existing beliefs.

The Secret Message

Out of all of the chapters I have written yet, I knew this would be the hardest to write. It's like a poem to some degree, but to most people it will seem dull. Congratulate me later after you realize that you made the mistake of reading this on the surface. Reading it without ever finding the hidden message, which is obviously the reason for the chapter.

Obviously the secret is out. Look closely and the message below the surface will show itself in obvious clarity. I hope you figure this out, so the efforts of this chapter do not go unrewarded. I think that would be the biggest waste.

The message that you'll find, be it interesting, is not something that even requires that this chapter make any sense. That's why you are about to read sentences that have no meaning, whatsoever. Flowing sentences have been used until now, but don't be fooled by their idiotically cryptic meanings going into the messages ahead.

That's why I'm donating money, food, labor, goods, services, gifts, blood, and time to whoever needs it to survive. You see? Behold: the sentence a child might write. Clearly, if not for selfish motivations, pride, status, or obvious profit gained, one might think the whole system is rigged carefully in my interest and the interest of those for which I care greatly. It is time to think about more than ourselves.

People like you are the reason why some caterpillars shouldn't turn into butterflies. Better they should donate their cocoons to other bugs whose blood, sweat, and tears are shed daily for those living the life of a free species.

I was afraid that up until now, I might have to keep people from finding the answers. However, I can safely assume that most readers didn't receive the will to find the secret. It was just a chapter of nonsense, for which they skipped over, looking for free advice somewhere else.

No luck there.

The Final Chapter.

Let me be the first to congratulate you on reading this WHOLE thing! Or at least skipping chapters you didn't like until you reached this one: THE FINAL CHAPTER!

A quick note about the title of this chapter: The Final Chapter isn't some kind of symbolic title that represents that this book is my final work. Oh, no, I plan to keep making books. This is fun. No, THE FINAL CHAPTER should be taken at face-value, which is that it's just the final chapter of this book.

Sure, there are "Acknowledgments" and an "About the Author" section after this chapter, so yeah, there is still a tiny chunk of pages to go.

However, before I get into the meat-and-potatoes of THE FINAL CHAPTER, I just want to take a quick second to ask you, the reader, what you think of this type of book. Are you interested in writing a book like this? Can I be of some help? I'd like to see more books like this one, and if you're flirting with the idea of making your own, I'd love to help. Reach out to me. I have contact information on the copyright page at the beginning of the book. Let's talk. I have no other motivations to help you besides the fact that I don't really care for super long books with long serious chapters, so I'd like to help you so that more books exist that I enjoy reading.

Okay, moving on.

Right now you might be thinking one of two thoughts:

1. "That's it? Well, that was a pretty short book."
   ...or...
2. "Thank God it's finally over! I was about to quit."

The Final Chapter.

If you're wondering about the size of the book, let me say, "So was I." When I wrote my first book, I was really trapped between two thoughts:

1. Will people really want to read ALL of this garbage?
2. Is my book bulky enough to be a "real book?"

The answer to the first was that people can quit or skip whatever they want, so the length doesn't really matter. The answer to the second was that any book is a real book.

But I'll be real with you. I wanted the hardcover and paperback to LOOK like a book. Not a tiny book or a mega book, but a normal sized book. I googled a lot to try and find some clear-cut answer to the question "how long should my book be?" There was no clear answer, but the most common one was "50,000 words, give or take, or whatever."

The problem with word quotas is… oh wait, I don't need to talk about this. I already covered this in the intro! So anyhow, page count mattered to me, even though page count didn't really matter to anyone. I wanted to make the book as short as I could while still making it feel like a normal-sized book.

UNCREDIBLE THOUGHTS

I took a book that I thought looked normal. I slid my finger along the side, flipping the back pages against the back cover, trying to find that magic spot where there were exactly ENOUGH pages. Just a hair more than "not enough," but far below "plenty." I did this a few times and got different answers each time. Get this: one time it was 212-pages, the next time it was 108-pages, and then multiple times in a row it was 160-pages. Here is where it gets weird:

- 160 is exactly halfway between 108 and 212
- Books being printed by Amazon that are under 108 pages all cost the same, and once you go over 108 pages you pay extra per page.

If this isn't a clear sign for a 108-page minimum, I don't know what is.

I've almost defined what will make a satisfactory book in my mind, but I do have to come back to "word count" for a second. You see, some people don't consider fewer than 25,000 words to be a full sized book. I noticed this when I was looking to nominate my book for contests. A 25k-word minimum showed up as a requirement more than once.

My pro-writer friend, Niki, would later tell me that something around 25,000 words is usually considered

The Final Chapter.

a Novella. Okay, whatever. None of this matters, right? Maybe to some, but I knew what I wanted. If there are people who consider fewer than 25k words to be too short for a book, and I had decided that 108 pages was my minimum, then I had defined my requirements for a book: it must be more than 25k words and more than 108 pages.

Right about now I bet you're realizing that THE FINAL CHAPTER might have ulterior motives. Yes, I wanted to conclude this book of random essays with a clear flickering of the lights and the announcement "you don't have to go home, but you can't read here." However, it is also a blatant vain attempt to add a few extra words and pages to this thing. I thought you would appreciate that I did this all in one place: THE FINAL CHAPTER! I didn't try to fluff up the other chapters with bullshit.

Since we're dealing with complete transparency, I don't feel guilty wasting space with these suggestions I received for this book on Facebook:

- **A request for illustrations:** I hope there were enough included to satisfy you. I paid an artist to make them, so I hope you appreciate them, asshole.

- **Any mention of Mexico:** I would like to go to Mexico someday. I'd like to eat Mexican food that isn't Americanized. However, my major concern with that is my lack of tolerance for hot peppers. A single seedless jalapeno added to a large pot of food might be too hot for me. But I would love me some fish tacos and a margarita. I can get that at the Greek-owned restaurant one mile from my house, though. But what I can't see are wild iguanas! And Mayan temples! I'm sorry if that makes me basic AF. I am who I am: Soy la tortuga de la muerte con queso.

- **Any mention of Dwayne Johnson:** You know that movie that Dwayne Johnson did with Mark Wahlberg where they are body-building criminals? I think it was called "Pain and Gain." That movie was pretty good, I think. I can't really remember. My movie review goes as follows: "Good, but not super memorable."

- **Address the struggles of lesbian mermaids and the fishing industry:** No. You're quoting this from somewhere, right? I tried googling it and I can't find it. If this is an original thought, kudos to you.

The Final Chapter.

- **Tips for eating two pounds of guacamole:** Tip #1 is to show up to the challenge with an empty stomach. Tip #2 is to make sure there are no hot peppers in it. Tip #3 is to make sure your mouth doesn't write checks your ass can't cash… like saying something to the effect of "No amount of guacamole is too much guacamole."
- **Multiple requests for a choose-your-own-adventure:** Sorry, not this book. However, I hope you enjoyed the "choose-your-own-feminism" worksheet in the chapter "Everyone Is A Feminist Until Proven Jerks."
- **A telling of the story "To Iowa And Back: 36-Hours of Magic (My Life On The Road With My Hero Tim)."** There isn't a lot to tell. I went on a road trip to Iowa with my hero, Tim. We saw some metalcore bands play in a bar. We ate Chinese food. We looked at records in a record store. Our hotel room was way too nice for lowlifes like us. I talked way too much as I often do. We spent a day hanging out with Ryan Morgan of the band Misery Signals. He choked the shit out of Tim. I photographed it. Then we all had coffee at a pleasant cafe. I pooped in a gas station bathroom, and it was magical.

- **A request for a scratch-and-sniff book:** I wish it could be. May I suggest turning to your favorite page of the book, and placing onto it a single drop of vanilla extract? Then, go to your least favorite page of the book, and pour melted candle wax all over it. Make sure it's the worst smelling candle you can find. That way your book will have a mixture of scents, and if you ever want to relive your least favorite page, you can scratch the wax off like a lottery ticket. It's the lottery where you're always a loser!

- **A request for step-by-step instructions for repairing a car engine's timing-belt:** Sure, no problem! First, what you're going to want to do is access a phone or tablet with an internet connection that reaches your vehicle. Next, go to a search engine website, such as Google. Last, type the make and model after the following quote "replace engine timing belt." You will be provided with instructions in the form of text, illustrations, videos, or likely all of the above. It's an amazing time to be alive. All that said, it once took me several hours to disconnect rusty connectors from my car battery, so all the knowledge in the world is no substitute for help from someone with hands-on experience (if you're on a time-crunch).

The Final Chapter.

As I said before, all the chapters (except this one) have no added bullshit to bulk them up. They are all organic in size. All the fluff is right here. Or, I should say, there it was and there it goes. We're past it.

Thank you for reading. I love you.

Sincerely,

John Marszalkowski

AKA Johnny, Johnny Too Hotty, Johnny Biceps, Johnny Chach Bag, Johnny Marshmallow, Johnny Marsz, Johnny Edward Marszałkowski, John John Leprechaun Went To School With Nothin' On, Doctor Optimus Prime, John Edward (only if i'm in trouble), Daddy, Charlotte's Dad, June's Dad, Desiree's Husband, and Hey You.

The End.

Acknowledgments

Thank you to everyone who bought this book.

Extra special thanks to everyone who bought this book AND my first book.

High-fives for the people who helped me make this book.

Nod of approval for anyone borrowing it from a library.

Squinting looks of disapproval for anyone who pirated it.

Confused looks of internal conflict for those of you who enthusiastically read it but bought it used, borrowed it from a friend, or received a promotional copy. I saw no revenue from your experience, but your expressive enthusiasm could lead to word-of-mouth sales. Time will tell. Money isn't the most important thing in life, right? It's nice, but I suppose it's more important to me that you enjoyed reading it. No matter what, you and I are buds.

Hugs, adoration, and kneeling worship to those of you who review this book. Be it on the review section of the website you bought it from, on your blog, social media, or orally at the water cooler.

About The Author

A typical day in the life of John Marszalkowski includes:

- Making eggs with too much cheese for breakfast and putting too much creamer in his coffee.
- Watching Disney movies with his daughter, Charlotte.
- Writing his next book
- Eating a bean burrito for lunch
- Cleaning up a tiny fraction of his messy house
- Writing music for his next album
- Feeding two dogs and a cat
- Taking Charlotte to the Milwaukee Zoo, the Milwaukee Public Museum, or the gym's childcare.
- Eating [redacted due to shame] for dinner.
- Researching his family tree
- Wasting massive amounts of time on social media
- Promoting his podcast, "Who Are We To Podcast?"

- Watching either The Office, Parks & Recreation, or 30 Rock for the millionth time.
- Dreaming about his wife, Desiree.

UNCREDIBLE THOUGHTS is the second book he has written, but the third book he has published (yeah, it's weird). If you enjoyed it, please check out his first book, *BUY MY BOOK: NOT BECAUSE YOU SHOULD, BUT BECAUSE I'D LIKE SOME MONEY*. Keep an eye out for his second published book, *HOW TO PUNCH KIDS IN BATHROOMS*. All are available everywhere dumb books are sold.

Oh, speak of the devil...

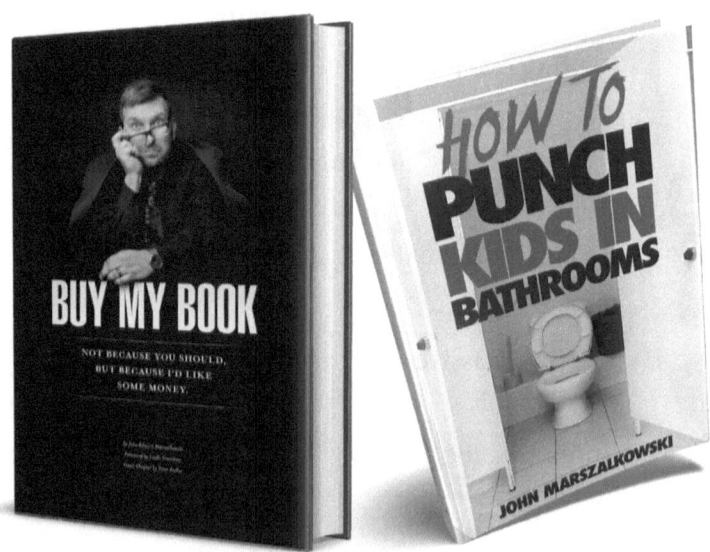

www.ingramcontent.com/pod-product-compliance
Lightning Source LLC
Chambersburg PA
CBHW030326080526
44584CB00012B/734